Date Due

NOV 2 5 '98			
6·2·99			
DEC 1 4 '99			
MAY 1 3 2000			
DEC 1 0 2001			
MAY 1 0 2002			
NOV 1 0 2004			
MAR 1 3 2007			

Cross-Cultural Practice

Cross-Cultural Practice

Assessment, Treatment, and Training

Sharon-ann Gopaul-McNicol, Ph.D.
Janet Brice-Baker, Ph.D.

John Wiley & Sons, Inc.

New York • Chichester • Weinheim • Brisbane • Singapore • Toronto

This text is printed on acid-free paper.

This publication is designed to provide accurate and authoritative
information in regard to the subject matter covered. It is sold
with the understanding that the publisher is not engaged in
rendering professional services. If legal, accounting, medical,
psychological, or any other expert assistance is required, the
services of a competent professional person should be sought.

Library of Congress Cataloging-in-Publication Data:

Gopaul-McNicol, Sharon-ann.
    Cross-cultural practice : assessment, treatment, and training /
Sharon-ann Gopaul-McNicol, Janet Brice-Baker.
        p.   cm.
    Includes bibliographical references and index.
    ISBN 0-471-14849-0 (alk. paper)
    1. Cultural psychiatry.   2. Ethnopsychology.   3. Minorities—
Mental health services.   4. Cross-cultural counseling.
    5. Intercultural communication.   I. Brice-Baker, Janet.   II. Title.
    RC455.4.E8G669   1998
    616.89—dc21   97-8869

Printed in the United States of America

10 9 8 7 6 5 4 3 2 1

To our families
Ulric, Monique Mandisa, Monica, Dale, and Adam

With gratitude and love and in
loving memory of our parents
St. Elmo Gopaul, Marian and Thomas Brice

Preface

T HIS BOOK IS the culmination of 12 years of cross-cultural practice, training, consultation, supervision, teaching, and research with families of various ethnic and cultural backgrounds. As we served these families both as practitioners and as consultants, we came to realize that a more comprehensive approach to assessment and intervention is needed for practitioners to adequately address the needs of families from diverse cultural backgrounds.

This book discusses or illustrates several models—the bio-ecological model to assessment, the Multicultural/Multimodal/Multisystems (Multi-CMS) model to treatment, and a cross-cultural competency model to training. These models and techniques were culled from the theories of cross-cultural psychology, the works of known cross-cultural practitioners and experts, and the present authors' practice, teaching, and research. These models suggest a more eclectic approach to assessment, treatment, and training practices in multicultural settings.

This book is divided into four parts. Part One examines historical assumptions of the influence of culture in the training of mental health workers (Chapter 1). This chapter also gives a wake-up call to the mental health field with respect to the need for an ethical mandate to examine alternatives to traditional assessment and counseling techniques.

Part Two begins by exploring assessment issues as they apply to culturally diverse children (Chapter 2). The best practices in report writing for the linguistically and culturally different client are also examined. Chapter 3 focuses on issues in cross-cultural assessment and its applicability for culturally diverse parents. Chapter 4 highlights ways of assessing culturally diverse couples.

Part Three presents treatment issues (Chapter 5) that can arise when working with culturally diverse families. Chapter 6 proposes a model—

Multi-CMS—approach to treatment that was developed by the primary author.

Part Four offers training suggestions for professors (Chapter 7) and clinical supervisors (Chapter 8). A comprehensive cross-cultural competency instrument is proposed in Chapter 9. Finally, Chapter 10 discusses implications for future research and clinical work, as well as a new vision for the mental health field.

SHARON-ANN GOPAUL-McNICOL

JANET BRICE-BAKER

Acknowledgments

T O OUR IMMEDIATE family, Ulric, Dale, Monique Mandisa, and
Adam, we extend our most profound gratitude. Your love, patience, and unflagging support throughout this challenging
time will be remembered in our hearts forever.

To our parents and other dear family members, the Gopauls, Brices,
and Hamptons, who instilled in us a sense of confidence and pride
about "being the best you can be," whose value for education brought
us to this point, and whose teachings both in word and deed really
breathe life into the saying, "the color of the balloon does not determine how high it will go." To you we extend much gratitude, respect,
and tenderness.

To our siblings, Gail, Wendy, Kurt, and Nigel Gopaul; Richard Brice
and Joanne Julius; our nieces and nephews, Michael, Kja, Michelle,
Skyler, and Kris; our cousins, Doreen, Christopher, and Maria, we
thank you for your ongoing support and patience.

To our professional family and colleagues who have helped to nur-
ture a respect for cross-cultural training, we thank you immensely:
Eleanor Armour-Thomas, Nancy Boyd-Franklin, A. J. Franklin, Freder-
ick Harper, Veronica Thomas, Beverly Greene, Lillian Comas-Diaz,
Louise Silverstein, Cheryl Thompson, Duncan Walton, Dean Lawrence
Siegel, Irma Hilton, Meyer Rothberg, Constance Ellison, Mary Conoley,
James Williams, Tania Thomas, Nicola Beckles, Aldrena Mabry, Emilia
Lopez, Grace Elizalde, Sara Nahari, Giselle Esquivel, Colleen Clay,
Miriam Azaunce, Lauraine Casella, Arthur Dozier, Joseph Cesar,
George Irish, Delroy Louden, Michael Barnes, Monica McGoldrick,
Paulette Moore Hines, John Pearce, Joseph Giordano, Denise Dartigue,
Emery Francois, Melvon Swanston, Jefferson Fish, Alina Camacho-
Gingerich, Willard Gingerich, Tony Bonaparte, Earl George, Joya

Gomez, Charmaine Edwards, Headley Wilson, Susan Lokai, Seretse McHardy, Koreen Seabrun, Sandra Hosein, Jennifer D'Ade, and Joanne Julien.

To the many students, interns, and clients who taught us about differences and whose lives help to conceptualize our philosophical and clinical position, we extend our gratitude.

To the communities and students of Howard University, Yeshiva University, St. John's University, Trinbago Networking Connection, and the California School of Professional Psychology–Los Angeles, we thank you for your support in the nurturing of this project.

To our deceased loved ones—St. Elmo Gopaul, Marian and Thomas Brice, Josephine Fritzgerald, and Julia Vane—may God bless you all.

We thank the permissions departments of Guilford Press, Greenwood Publishing Group, Sage Publications, Allyn & Bacon, and John Wiley for granting permission to use segments of our own work from journal articles and book chapters.

This project would not have been possible without the tremendous editorial assistance of Kelly Franklin and Tracey Thornblade of John Wiley & Sons.

Contents

HISTORICAL ASSUMPTIONS ABOUT THE INFLUENCE OF CULTURE IN THE TRAINING OF MENTAL HEALTH WORKERS

CHAPTER 1

Historical and Philosophical Assumptions in Cross-Cultural Training

A Wake-Up Call to the Profession

PSYCHOLOGY, SINCE its origin, has been strongly influenced by culture. This is because psychotherapy, in and of itself, does not take place in a vacuum independent of the sociopolitical influences of the larger society. Culture represents the values, customs, beliefs, heritage, and norms of a particular group of people from a society. The transmission of certain social values from one generation to another is observed through the cultural processes. This chapter will first present a brief history of cross-cultural psychology and a definition of culture and then will attempt to highlight the impact of culture on the mores and customs of cross-ethnic/cultural populations.

Cross-cultural psychology has a long-established history that is not unique to the American culture. Around the world, people are aware of how difficult it is to communicate with those from different cultural backgrounds. Given the history of cross-cultural relations, one can expect this situation to continue as long as people are racially, linguistically, culturally, religiously, and politically different. The challenge for

3

Americans is to address not only our differences as people, but the sentiment that the traditions, values, and beliefs of people different from the dominant majority are inferior. History has shown that the ease with which immigrants have assimilated in the United States depends upon their race and cultural similarity to the dominant group (Ponterotto, Casas, Suzuki, & Alexander, 1995).

In the late 1950s and early 1960s, culturally diverse therapists expressed concern that many mainstream mental health professionals "do not accept, respect and understand cultural differences" (Pine, 1972, p. 35). This is because mental health professionals, as any other group in a society, are raised according to that society's social norms. Thus, they may define the "normal" family according to the cultural and social norms to which they are accustomed. The implicit assumptions in the definitions were often never examined by mental health workers in the context of the culturally different client.

By the early 1970s, multicultural counseling had become a buzzword in the psychology literature because the counseling profession had come to recognize that the techniques being implemented were inadequate for working with culturally different people. Questions regarding the validity of the existing theories and techniques emerged with vigor among culturally diverse practitioners, which led to a more comprehensive perspective in counseling.

In the 1990s, multiculturalism, which encapsulates all groups represented in the United States, has become the "fourth force" in psychology and education. The issue that we now face as we approach the new millennium is how our curricula, clinical practice, and research methodologies will reflect this diversity.

DEFINITION AND CONCEPTUALIZATION OF CULTURE

Evans-Pritchard (1962) captures the true spirit of cultural differences in his representation of the Christian and Muslim faiths: "A Christian man shows respect for his religion by taking off his hat but keeping on his shoes, while a Muslim man in an Arab country will show similar respect by keeping on his hat and removing his shoes" (p. 2). Frisby (1992) and Mosley-Howard (1995) offered various definitions of culture, such as the one stated in the next paragraph. For the purposes of this book, we define culture as a way of living that encompasses the customs, traditions, attitudes, and overall socialization in which a group of people engage that are unique (not deficient) to their cultural upbringing.

By this definition of culture, it is evident that a multicultural perspective provides an opportunity for two persons from different cultural backgrounds to have divergent views without one being perceived as right and superior and the other as wrong and inferior. In other words, a multicultural perspective tolerates and even supports diverse views of mental health. It takes a broad view of culture, incorporating education, religion, ethnicity, language, nationality, gender, age, geographic location, and socioeconomic factors. Therefore, one's cultural identity is dynamic, constantly evolving as one moves from one context to another (Pedersen, 1985, 1995).

BARRIERS TO THE MULTICULTURAL MOVEMENT

Everyone is born with the capacity to be tolerant of people from different cultural orientations. However, the sociocultural environment can impose barriers that impede the development of cultural flexibility. Ramirez (1991) outlines three major barriers to the formulation of an environment of diversity: pressures to conform, racial prejudice, and oppression. In general, all three are represented in the messages conveyed by the various institutions in society and by the family.

PRESSURES TO CONFORM

Many culturally different individuals have experienced pressure to reject their culture's values and customs and adopt the dominant society's cultural styles. Refusal to do so could result in tacit punishments, such as limited access to programs that aid in the empowerment of the individual or family. Pressure also comes in the form of mythical ideals, such as that light-skinned people are more attractive than dark-skinned people; the result can be feelings of inferiority by those whose skin color is dark. Likewise, reference to a southern or foreign accent as being less appealing than a northern accent has led to feelings of insecurity, refusal to communicate, or pressure to change one's accent for fear of being ostracized. To say the least, these mythical ideals prevent everyone in society from respecting and benefiting from diversity.

RACIAL PREJUDICE

Race has played a critical role in the economic, social, and political structure of American society from its precolonial beginnings to the present (Carter, 1995). Racism, prejudice, and discrimination are moderator variables emanating from the larger society or majority group that have a direct impact on the acculturation process (Aponte & Van Deusen, 1981). Racism can be external to the family and experienced as discrimination, or internalized in a sense of shame about oneself (Boyd-Franklin, 1989). Racism can be expressed in two ways: attitudinal and structural. Bem (1974) defined attitude as a positive or negative evaluation of people, objects, ideas, or events. Attitudinal racism can lead the mainstream or majority culture to behave toward ethnic groups by teasing, labeling, scapegoating, neglecting, and denying equal opportunity and equal rights (Aponte & Van Deusen, 1981). Institutional racism involves a pattern of rules, regulations, and behaviors that are exclusionary and exploitive and are part of an organization or social system (Aponte & Van Deusen, 1981). Prejudice refers to a negative attitude toward or evaluation of a person due solely to his or her membership in a group; a stereotype is a set of beliefs about the characteristics of people in a particular group that is generalized to include almost all group members (Carter, 1995).

Racism contributes immensely to how a culture evolves in the mainstream society and how culturally different people assimilate to the group. Racism affects the immigrant's work, self-esteem, and interpersonal relationships. For example, Gopaul-McNicol (1993) indicated that racial self-perception plays an important role in the overall adjustment of immigrants of color from the West Indies. Those who perceived themselves as Blacks before they migrated tended to adjust more easily with respect to the European or American definition of Black. Those who perceived themselves as White (people of mixed descent: European and African, and East Indians) usually went through a period of denial when they were termed Black by the European and American societies. Likewise, healthy cultural paranoia engendered in African

Americans as a consequence of experiencing racism and prejudice has been identified, and involves a general distrust and suspicion of majority institutions (Aponte & Van Deusen, 1981).

Through prejudicial practices, those who hold the power in society prevent those who are different from securing equal status. The powerful message is that if a person is different because of gender, race, religion, and so on, he or she is not likely to attain the same level of success as those who are more alike. Prejudice can be very limiting and destructive to the development of a positive cultural diversity sentiment because it keeps people separate and it exploits the fears and stereotypes of individuals.

OPPRESSION

Oppression (which involves cruel and unjust use of power) is even more of an impediment than the other two barriers. There is not only pressure to be what one is not, but oppression prevents one from participating in the dominant society's activities. Exploitation (which involves unethical use of something or someone) is also part of an oppressive system.

A WAKE-UP CALL TO THE MENTAL HEALTH FIELD

The U.S. population of Anglo ancestry will constitute no more than 50% by the year 2050 (U.S. Census, 1989). The kaleidoscope of ethnic populations in the United States is a result of migration and political instability in many developing nations (U.S. Census, 1989). There is no doubt that this increasing diversity of cultures has created challenges for social, education, and health institutions in the United States.

In the 1960s, when humanism became a third force in psychology to supplement the psychodynamic and behavioral perspectives, it was initially received with much ambivalence and trepidation. Today, it is widely accepted. In the same manner, cross-cultural psychology has been a source of controversy and anxiety among mainstream psychologists in the United States. The source of greatest anxiety may be the concern that this is an area on which White psychologists are not going to be able to hold a monopoly. Whatever the currently prevailing issues, mental health professionals are recognizing that cross-cultural psychology will be an important factor as we move into the twenty-first century.

WHAT DO WE DO TO STAY VIBRANT AS A DISCIPLINE?

If psychology as a profession is going to endure in a growing multiethnic, multicultural society, and if psychology is to receive acceptance from the culturally different, it must begin to demonstrate its ability, commitment, and good faith to contribute to the betterment of life for all people. This can be addressed in a variety of ways.

First, psychology has to confront the politics of its profession. Issues in assessment and counseling are not morally and politically neutral. This attitude has only resulted in the subjugation of ethnically and culturally diverse people and the continued belief that these individuals are inferior intellectually and are pathological. The psychology profession can no longer be excused for its passivity toward the inequities in the social system.

Second, as a profession, psychology must begin to examine more critically what constitutes normalcy and what harmful assumptions are inherent in psychology training programs. In this book, we are forcefully calling for the inclusion of cross-cultural competencies throughout the graduate training of psychology majors. Chapter 7 discusses such a curriculum in detail. In addition, the American Psychological Association (APA) should mandate that all training programs infuse such curricula throughout the course of study. In other words, the study of ethnically and culturally different clients ought to receive equal attention and fair representation.

Third, a pluralistic perspective in psychology should have at its center questions pertaining to the validity of the current theories and strategies in the psychology profession. This is needed because the existing mainstream techniques and theories have been found to be ineffective in working with ethnically and culturally different families.

Fourth, psychology programs need to be more aggressive in attracting not only a more equitable distribution of minority students, but minority professors as well. Culturally different students and professors can counterbalance cultural misrepresentations by offering different perspectives from the traditional Anglo-Saxon teaching model. Along this vein, there is a need to shift research energies from the pathological, intellectually deficient ethnically and culturally different client to the psychologically healthy, intellectually high-functioning ethnically and culturally different client.

Finally, it is critical to recognize that culture pervades the lives of every person in one form or another. Culture forces a vibrant relationship between the personality of an individual and the social context in which he or she interacts. As a result, the roles people play and the normative behaviors expected of them must be interpreted from an ecological perspective, that is, through the culture in which they function. What may be deviant or anomalous in one culture may be healthy and acceptable in another. The United States is presently the most culturally diverse country in the world (Comas-Diaz & Griffith, 1988), and American clinicians need to be more attuned to the notion that mental health services to ethnically diverse populations must be delivered in a culturally relevant manner.

PART TWO

ASSESSMENT AND CULTURE

CHAPTER 2

Assessment of Children

A CULTUROLOGICAL APPROACH
TO PERSONALITY ASSESSMENT

ALTHOUGH THERE is a vast body of literature on the topic of psychopathology, considerably less literature exists on its cross-cultural manifestations, in particular as it applies to children. Over the past 10 years, cross-cultural mental health workers have raised concern about the validity of Westernized diagnostic criteria for immigrants as a group. Many books on psychopathology assume that across cultures and across populations, people manifest psychiatric distress similarly. However, evidence from cross-cultural studies of depression and other mental disorders suggest otherwise (Marsella et al., 1973; Tseng et al., 1986). The *DSM-IV*, unlike its predecessors, attempts to address specific cultural factors endemic to cross-cultural populations. In general, clinicians have to be culturally sensitive to the fact that the manifestation and acceptance of these disorders are dependent upon cultural values (Draguns, 1987). For instance, in non-Western societies, mood (e.g., depression) and anxiety disorders are more prevalent and accepted than personality and thought disorders (Gopaul-McNicol, 1993). In most "third-world" countries, psychosomatic complaints such as physical aches, pains, dizziness, upset stomach, gas problems (mainly reported in the stomach), and nerves are more acceptable and more commonly reported. Often, these psychosomatic complaints are masking a depressive type of disorder that the individual, for cultural reasons, is unable to talk about. The reason physical complaints are more accepted than psychological ones is because most people around the world have not conceptualized psychotherapy in the same manner as Westerners have. Besides, physical complaints elicit compassion, whereas psychological complaints result in a judgment of weakness and failure, especially toward males. Thus, secondary gains may be achieved because these ailments relieve the person of responsibility. Generally, the stresses include academic difficulties, social problems, school phobias, and so on. The response is usually in the form of physical and psychological symptoms that result in psychosomatic ailments, such as heart weakness, asthma, bodily aches, digestive problems, sleep disturbance, depression, and anxiety disorders.

An examination of the most commonly diagnosed childhood mental disorders will be discussed in this chapter, with an emphasis on various culturological factors to consider.

COMMONLY DIAGNOSED PSYCHOPATHOLOGICAL DISORDERS AMONG CULTURALLY DIVERSE CHILDREN

In mental hospitals in the United States, anxiety has been reported as the most frequent complaint among culturally diverse children and adolescents, and depression has been noted as the second most commonly diagnosed psychopathology (Kashani et al., 1987). Childhood disruptive disorders such as Attention Deficit Hyperactivity Disorder (ADHD), Oppositional Defiant Disorder, and Conduct Disorder continue to be the most widely reported mental disorders among children in school settings. Before discussing these disorders and their culture-specific factors, it is necessary to examine two commonly found risk factors that may lead to the development of emotional disorders: immigration and family role changes.

One potential source of stress for the immigrant client is *immigration* itself. For some, the very reason for leaving their countries and the means by which they had to leave results in traumatic reactions. The components of stress come from having to flee one's native country because of persecution, often abruptly, possibly with no chance to say good-bye to loved ones, with no opportunity to plan, no means of bringing belongings on the trip, and living in constant fear of discovery.

Another considerable source of stress for immigrants, regardless of their reason for migration, is leaving family members behind. Sometimes anxiety symptoms are not even present until after the family is reunited. Having lived through separation in the past makes any future separation, real or imagined, a toxic issue (Brice, 1982). Once an entire family or individual has successfully made connections in the United States and established a home, other risk factors must be considered during evaluation and therapy. For example, adjustment disorder with anxious mood is a consideration when assessing reactions to a new home, a new physical environment, strange foods, and an unfamiliar climate.

A second risk factor for emotional disorder in these children is *family role changes.* Unlike in Western societies, such as the United States where nuclear families operate independently (Saeki & Borow, 1987; Sue & Zane, 1987; Triandis, 1987), in most countries around the world, the nuclear family is part of the extended family. To a large extent, relationships with neighbors and institutions such as the place of worship and the school are perceived as collective and familylike, rather than in individualistic terms (Gopaul-McNicol, 1993; Thrasher & Anderson, 1988; Triandis, 1987). Likewise, whereas in Western societies egalitarian structures of power are nurtured and individualistic pursuit of happiness and fulfillment are emphasized (Gushue & Sciarra, 1995; Kim, 1985; Sloan, 1990), in most culturally diverse families, individual desires are suppressed, replaced by those of the family and even of the society. Besides, in many "third-world" countries, relationships are hierarchical and power is dependent upon age and gender (Gopaul-McNicol, 1993). Parents and elders are well respected in these societies, unlike in North America, where youth takes precedence over the aged. Loyalty and respect for one's elders are emphasized to the extent that it is disrespectful to discuss negative feelings about one's parents to a stranger. Moreover, children are socialized to have a relational-value, community-type orientation, with a focus more on societal commitment than individual development (Brice, 1982; Gopaul-McNicol, 1993). Thus, an individual who pursues his or her own personal interest and forsakes the family's goals is perceived as self-centered and avaricious. The self is defined more with respect to the roles the individual plays in the community and the family and is conceived less in individualistic terms. Because of this modus operandi, interpersonal and intrafamilial boundaries are not as clearly defined as they are in North America, and the need for privacy is seen as selfish.

Family therapists often get referrals when the family has been reunited. Such reunification calls into question family roles and family loyalty. Minuchin (1974) has stressed the importance of maintaining optimal family structure. Every family has a structure that provides family members with a blueprint for how to behave and knowledge of what is expected of them. It specifies gender roles (male and female) and generational roles (grandparents, parents, children). Minuchin and other structural family therapists contend that when a structure is altered (e.g., boundaries between generations get blurred or members of one generation assume the duties of another generation), it gives rise to anxiety in the family. The precipitator for the change in structure, the gradualness or abruptness of the change, and the family's accommodation to it are just some of the factors that may influence who becomes the symptom carrier (i.e., the family member who develops a clinical disorder).

In assessing the emotional adjustment of immigrant children in the schools, it is necessary to examine the normal acculturation problems that any immigrant child can experience upon entry into the U.S. school system. In making a healthy adjustment to a new school, immigrant children will first tend to draw on their cultural background as a form of reference, in the same way that kindergarten students draw on their home experiences. Because immigrant children are often initially left behind with relatives while their parents get settled and established in this country, when they first arrive, many are readjusting to their parents after several years of separation. During this period, children become quite attached to their caretakers, whom they come to know as their parents. When these children are reunited with their parents, conflicts arise around such issues as family relations, discipline, and culture. Conflicts also emerge when children are at different adaptation phases than their parents. Immigrant children can face overwhelming problems in school as they contend with the cultural clash between the norms of their native country and expectations in the host country (Goodstein, 1990). In addition, immigrants typically come from homogeneous nations; they are accustomed neither to racial and ethnic diversity nor to the racism found in the United States. It is therefore common for them to experience confusion and cultural conflict. As a general practice, mental health workers ought to conduct culturological assessment of immigrant clients to avoid misdiagnosis.

Several types of misdiagnosis can result because of these cultural clashes. For school-age children, anxiety disorders such as Posttraumatic Stress Disorder (PTSD), depression, and childhood disruptive disorders—in particular, ADHD and schizophrenia—are the most common misdiagnoses (Gopaul-McNicol, 1993), and therefore, these will be highlighted in the next section.

Posttraumatic Stress Disorder or Emotional Disturbance?

When natural disasters, such as hurricanes, or the ongoing political unrest in many "third-world" countries precipitate their immigration, many children enter the United States traumatized. Thomas (1991) has discussed the responses to trauma in terms of the age of the children. In summarizing the literature, she stated that "the intrusion of memories and thoughts connected to the traumatic event can cause the child to be distracted from an academic task" (p. 5). Ronstrom (1989) found that some children become hysterical at the sound of loud noises. Thus, compounding the already stressful process of immigration, these children are faced with memories of violence and death. The behaviors exhibited by children in reaction to these stressors can range from withdrawal to aggression.

Mollica, Wyshak, and Lowelle (1987) emphasized that in spite of the profound stress that these traumatized victims experienced, they have difficulty articulating their trauma-related symptoms because the expression of these symptoms can significantly increase their emotional distress. The result can be poor academic work, behavioral problems in school, and more difficulty in acculturation. Unfortunately, these behaviors can be misdiagnosed as emotional disturbance. It is vital that psychologists allow children the time to acculturate and assist in directing families to supportive centers where they can receive educational and psychological services to aid in the cultural transition.

Adjustment Disorder or Depression?

Recently, there has been an increase in referrals of immigrant children due to the depression noted by school psychologists. Although it is important to be concerned about such symptoms as a lack of interest in social activities, feelings of worthlessness, and depressed mood, it is equally important to distinguish the *DSM-IV* criteria for a diagnosis of depression from the stages of acculturation that immigrant children go through. Many culturally diverse children who are referred by the school for therapy because of depressed mood are quite social at home and in their communities. In most countries around the world, children are taught to be quiet in the classroom; North American school officials often misinterpret their respect for the classroom setting as withdrawal, shyness, depression, and so forth. Many children say that they are amazed at the liberties that are accorded children in the American classroom. It takes time for them to get used to this liberal, unstructured approach. Simply observing these children on the playground should aid in ruling out shyness and withdrawal. A more appropriate diagnosis might be adjustment disorder with depressed mood, since many of these children do not continue to show signs of withdrawal for more than six months (according to the *DSM-IV*, an adjustment disorder cannot have a duration of longer than six months). In such patients, as opposed to those with more serious depression, the experience is transient, and suicidal ideation (if it exists at all) is likely to manifest itself more like an anxiety disorder. Helping the client cope with the anxieties and offering practical recommendations for dealing with life in the United States tend to have good results without resorting to pharmacological treatment. In addition, reassuring clients that their symptoms are probably transient and that therapist and client together can alleviate them will be useful.

Disruptive Disorders and Culture-Specific Factors

Attention Deficit Hyperactive Disorder.   Although ADHD is found across cultures, the interpretation of the behaviors and the variation in reporting procedures are probably what result in a lower reported incidence of hyperactivity from culturally diverse therapists.

Among ethnically and culturally diverse families, a child's excess activity is not perceived as negative, as it is sometimes perceived by the dominant Caucasian society. Ethnically and culturally diverse families encourage such "verve and high levels of sensate stimulation" (Allen & Boykin, 1992, p. 589). Among African Americans, for example, these dimensions grew out of Afro-cultural experiences that are "rooted in movement-expressive orientation" (p. 591) and that emphasize the interweaving of movements and the "juggling of several things at one time."

Allen and Boykin (1992) emphasized that "the most salient aspect of these children's lives are neither valued nor relevant to the academic arena," rendering them incongruent with the cultural ethos of the typical mainstream American classrooms. The authors offer a prescriptive pedagogy involving nine interrelated dimensions of the Afro-cultural experiences linking spiritual, communal, and oral characteristics central to the ethos of African people. The issues raised by these authors have been found to be common among children from culturally diverse backgrounds, and they ought to be considered in the same vein as the cultural integrity model proposed by the authors for African American children.

Conduct Disorder. The *DSM-IV* cautions clinicians to be sensitive to immigrant youths from war-torn countries who were involved in civil wars and therefore may show symptoms of aggression, which was necessary for their survival in their native countries. Such children would not warrant a diagnosis of Conduct Disorder given the sociopolitical and economic contexts in which the undesirable behaviors first occurred. Thus, consistent with all mental disorders, "the Conduct Disorder diagnosis should be applied only when the behavior in question is symptomatic of an underlying dysfunction within the individual and not simply a reaction to the immediate social context" (American Psychiatric Association, 1994, p. 88).

INTELLECTUAL ASSESSMENT:
A BIO-ECOLOGICAL APPROACH

There has long been a relationship between minority children and special education, as evidenced by the disproportionate numbers of minority and immigrant children placed into special education classes. This overrepresentation of ethnic and culturally different children in special education classes has been partially attributed to "the indiscriminate use of psychological tests, especially IQ tests" (Cummings, 1984, p. 1). The IQ test has legitimized the labeling of many minority children as "mentally retarded" and their resulting placement in special educational classes (Armour-Thomas, 1992; Boykin, 1983; Gopaul-McNicol, Black, & Castro, 1997; Helms, 1992; Mercer, 1979; Mowder, 1980; Oakland, 1977; Oakland & Phillips, 1973; Rodriguez-Fernandez, 1981;

Samuda, 1975, 1976; Tucker, 1980; Vasquez-Nuttall, 1987; Vasquez-Nuttall, Goldman, & Landurand, 1983). The objective of this section is to examine from a practical standpoint some alternatives to traditional psychological assessment for ethnically and culturally diverse students.

Armour-Thomas and Gopaul-McNicol (1997a, 1997b) emphasized that intelligence is a multifaceted set of abilities that can be enhanced depending on the social and cultural contexts in which it has been nurtured, crystallized, and ultimately assessed. The authors noted that when children were observed in familiar contexts such as their homes and in the company of familiar significant others, a heightened ability to perform the activity being assessed was found. Therefore, there is a need to expand the notions of intelligence that have been developed within the psychometric and information-processing traditions. This does not mean that information-processing theories and psychometric measures are not relevant in the field of intelligence. However, these theories need to be expanded to include a more cultural anthropological approach. The important point to note is that IQ is a quite labile concept, and thus contextual influences on more complex tasks inevitably cast doubt on current conceptualizations of intelligence. This notion of the ecological dependency of cognition stems from a basic principle within Vygotsky's (1978) sociohistorical perspective that nascent cognitive potentials emerge, develop, and are displayed within a sociocultural milieu. Vygotsky's sociohistorical perspective has guided much of the empirical research on cognition and development (see reviews by Ceci, 1990; Rogoff & Chavajay, 1995; Sternberg, Wagner, & Okagaki, 1993). Researchers in this tradition have sought an understanding of people's everyday cognition by examining their thinking in real-world tasks, in multiple real-world environments. What is remarkable about this body of work is that successful performance on these real-world tasks seems to require the same cognitive processes or strategies that are used in the successful performance on standardized intelligence tests. Yet, there is weak or no correlation between performance on both kinds of tasks. A more comprehensive explanation of the inseparability of context and cognition may be found in Ceci's (1990) bio-ecological treatise on intellectual development, Sternberg's (1986) triarchic theory of intelligence, and Armour-Thomas and Gopaul-McNicol's bio-ecological measures nested within their biocultural theoretical perspective. Each of these

authors takes the position that cognition is, in part, a culturally dependent construct. This is because, as human beings, we are born with diverse capacities that predispose us to engage in activities within any
given ecology. This line of thought has led us to conceive of intellectual
behavior as an inextricable biocultural phenomenon and argue for a bio-
ecological approach to intellectual assessment.

Armour-Thomas and Gopaul-McNicol (1997a) propose a flexible,
ecologically sensitive assessment system that allows for greater heterogeneity in the expression of intelligence. In short, they contend
that other qualitative, nonpsychometric approaches must complement
the quantitative psychometric measures of intelligence. A review of
the work of these authors will shed light on the understanding of the
best practice in intellectually assessing ethnically and culturally different children. A brief examination of this model is outlined in the
next section in a case example and is captured in Table 2.1.

The important point to remember is that there is no single psychometric measure that taps the three interrelated and dynamic dimensions
of intelligence: biological cognitive processes, culturally coded experiences, and cultural contexts. Therefore, any psychometric measure or
amalgamation of tests (interbattery testing, the process approach to
assessment, cross-battery testing) that emphasizes a score-oriented
approach should be used in conjunction with the following nonpsychometric ecological measures outlined in Armour-Thomas and Gopaul-
McNicol (in press):

Family/community support assessment
Other intelligences assessment
Item equivalency assessment measure
Test-Teach-Retest assessment measure
Ecological taxonomy of intellectual assessment
Teacher questionnaire

FAMILY/COMMUNITY SUPPORT ASSESSMENT

This is a questionnaire designed to determine what support systems the
child has at home and in the community, what has been the child's previous educational experiences, and what language is spoken at home.

Table 2.1

General Reminders for the 4-Tier Bio-Ecological
Assessment Report

When reporting the test results, include sections on:

1. *Psychometric Assessment*
   Even in this psychometric section, the report should be qualitative, for instance, describing the child's strengths and weaknesses in the constructs measured by each subtest.

2. *Psychometric Potential Assessment*
   This tier consists of four components:

   Suspending time

   Contextualizing vocabulary

   Paper and pencil

   Test-Teach-Retest

   This section reveals the child's potential/estimated intellectual functioning. If the child shows an improvement in performance, state so. Statements such as "Stephanie went from low average to average" should be emphasized.

3. *Ecological Assessment*
   This ecological taxonomy of intellectual assessment consists of four components:

   Family/community support assessment

   Observation to determine performance in the settings below (item/cultural equivalence)

   Stage of acculturation

   Teacher questionnaire

   These components are used to assess the child in three settings:

   School (classroom, gym, and playground)

   Home

   Community (place of worship, playground, and/or other recreational sites)

Table 2.1 (Continued)

In this section, a child is observed in his or her ecology: home, community, school. The examiner discusses all tasks that the child was able to perform in these settings, but not what the child was unable to do in the IQ testing situation, even under potential IQ assessment.

4. *Other Intelligences*
   This tier consists of four components:

   Musical intelligence

   Bodily/kinesthetic intelligence

   Interpersonal intelligence

   Intrapersonal intelligence

OTHER INTELLIGENCES ASSESSMENT

This measure attempts to capture two of Gardner's (1993) commonly found intelligences among culturally different children: musical and bodily/kinesthetic. In assessing culturally and linguistically different children, other intelligences must be examined because the IQ tests do not reflect all of the intelligences of an individual. Interviewing several persons (child, teacher, parent) is necessary to add reliability to the child's description of his or her other intelligences.

ITEM EQUIVALENCIES ASSESSMENT MEASURE

The item equivalency assessment measure attempts to equate a child's cultural experience in every item of every IQ test by matching the questions on the IQ test to the child's culture. Thus, the child's broad-based information repertoire is recognized. A caveat: it is not statistically possible to quantify cultural equivalence. However, powerful information can be obtained clinically. Thus, psychologists who consider themselves more than just psychometricians will still find this measure very helpful because they can create clinically a cluster of items that form the construct of intelligence for a particular cultural group.

Contextualization versus Decontextualization

While McGrew (1995) found that vocabulary is only moderately influenced by American culture, Hilliard's (1979) question "What precisely is meant by vocabulary?" is a valid one that advocates for IQ tests have not yet answered. Words have different meanings in different cultures. For instance, the Spanish translation of "banana," *tostone,* means a quarter or a half-dollar to a Chicano, and to a Puerto Rican, it means a squashed part of a banana that has been fried. It is important to allow the child to say the words in a sentence to be sure that the child's understanding of the word's meaning is the same as that on the English-language IQ test.

The important issue here is that vocabulary is contextually determined; that is, it is learned in everyday contexts rather than through direct instruction. Children accomplish this decontextualization by embedding unknown words in simple contexts. Children who did not know the word meanings in isolation were able to figure out the meanings when words were placed in a surrounding context. Of course, on traditional IQ tests, children are asked word meanings in isolation. Whereas this may be acceptable for children who have had adequate educational opportunities in adequate social environments, for children who come from educationally deprived environments, word definition without the surrounding context may lead to invalid findings of their intelligence, in particular, knowledge acquisition.

Armour-Thomas and Gopaul-McNicol (in press) recommend that the examiner can contextualize all words by asking the child to say them in a sentence. Credit is given only if the child (not the examiner) uses it correctly in a sentence.

Paper and Pencil on the Arithmetic Subtests

Arithmetic taps skill, memory/attention, and speed. In the standard procedure whereby the child is expected to solve the problem mentally, it is difficult to tell whether the child has the skill or not, or if it is the child's inability to sustain attention that may be impeding performance. Potential testing allows the examiner to rule out which factor is operating. For potential testing on the arithmetic subtest of the Wechsler scales, use paper and pencil and say to the child who fails, "Please use this paper and pencil and try to solve the problem." This response will fall under a potential score.

TEST-TEACH-RETEST ASSESSMENT MEASURE

While Esquivel (1985) emphasized that "performance scales of standardized intelligence tests appear to have the greatest predictive validity for Limited English Proficient students, and may provide a more accurate estimate of their actual abilities" (p. 119), the nonverbal subtests—contrary to the claims that have been espoused—are not culture-fair and are definitely not culture-free. In fact, it is "the information (direct experience) components of these tests that carry their culture-bound characteristics" (Cohen, 1969, p. 840; Feurstein, 1979; Lidz, 1991).

Because nonverbal tests rely on one's ability to reason logically, the most culture-bound way of cognitive processing is carried out in tests of logical thinking. The Block Design and Object Assembly subtests are highly influenced by American culture; therefore, American children will find the experience less novel and thus their performances will be more automatized. Hence, the tests will not be measuring the same skills across cultures and populations. Most children who are from rural areas in "third-world" countries have had little if any prior exposure to puzzles and blocks. Sternberg (1984) emphasized that these nonverbal subtests can be unfair for culturally diverse students. A fair comparison between groups would require equitable degrees of familiarity or novelty in test items, as well as comparable strategies. The average child who comes from such cultures is very handy, able to help in constructing buildings and making furniture, even though he or she has no formal education in these areas. These tasks are as or more complicated than putting blocks or puzzles together. Therefore, it would not be logical to label these children as delayed intellectually when they have honed other, more complicated nonverbal skills. In fact, when testing the limits of culturally different children on the nonverbal subtests, it is quite common for students to get the more difficult items correct after they have passed their ceiling points or after time limits have been met. It seems as if the children are learning as they go along, that lack of familiarity may be why they did not do as well on the earlier items. Unfortunately, by the time they understand how to manipulate the blocks and put the puzzles together, it is time to stop those particular subtests because they have already reached their ceiling point. Of course, in keeping with standardization procedures, one ought not to receive credit for items passed after the ceiling point has been attained.

Armour-Thomas and Gopaul-McNicol (in press) suggest that the *test-teach-retest* is only to be administered if the examiner realizes that the child was not exposed to these types of items prior to the testing, that is, if the child never played with blocks, puzzles, and so on. The authors suggest that the examiner teach the child and then retest. For instance, on the Block Design, Picture Arrangement, or Object Assembly subtests of the Wechsler scales, if a child fails the first item on both trials, teach the skill and give the test again. The examiner is to give credit under potential if the child performs successfully. The important point to remember is that the same procedures are followed as in the standardized testing, except time is suspended, teaching is done, and potential scores are given after the child passes the teaching items. (Please review Armour-Thomas & Gopaul-McNicol, in press, for a more extensive examination of these procedures and to peruse the additional questions that ought to be asked following the retest period.)

Suspending Time

The question of whether speeded timed tests are biased measures of intelligence for some ethnically and culturally different children is another critical issue and a shortcoming of most intelligence tests. The North American view that speed of mental functioning is a critical component of intelligence is based on the assumption that to be smart is to be quick. Many contemporary theorists (Brand & Deary, 1982; Carroll, 1993; Eysenck, 1982; Horn, 1991; Jensen, 1979; Woodcock-Johnson, 1990) based their theories on individual differences in the speed of information processing. Sternberg (1984) argues that although speed may be critical for some mental operations, "the issue ought not to be speed per se, but rather speed selection: knowing when to perform at what rate and being able to function rapidly or slowly depending on the tasks or situational demands" (p. 7). Thurstone (1924) emphasized that a critical factor of intelligence is the ability to substitute rapid, impulsive responses for rational, reflective ones. Noble (1969) found that children can be trained to increase their reaction time by teaching them to do so through automatic practice. Armour-Thomas & Gopaul-McNicol (in press) have found that the more the children practice, the faster is their reaction time.

It is important to note that while speed of mental functioning has been associated with intelligence testing, it is well known that snap judgments are not an important attribute of intelligence. Baron (1981, 1982) also noted that, with respect to problem solving, a reflective cognitive style is generally associated with intelligence. De Avila and Havassy (1974) noted that assessing culturally different children via timed tests confuses the measurement of ability with the measurement of aspiration, as little regard is given to children who are not culturally trained to work under timed conditions. Gopaul-McNicol (1993) found that most Caribbean children have difficulty completing tasks under time pressures because this represents the antithesis of what their culture dictates. On the contrary, slow and careful execution of their work is highly valued, so that even if the child is aware of being timed, he or she may ignore the request by the examiner for a quick response, and instead execute the work methodically and cautiously. Thus, scores tend to be lower for such students on timed tests, which comprise most of the nonverbal subtests. Of course, there are some professions, such as air traffic control, that require quick decisions. Speed is essential in such situations, but most events of everyday life do not require decision making in the few seconds typically allotted for problem solving on IQ tests. The important issue should not be one of total time spent, but time distribution across various kinds of processing and planning events. The practical point to be made from this is that students ought not to be penalized for not completing a task in the allotted time. Instead, they should be credited for successful completion of the task (Gopaul-McNicol & Armour-Thomas, 1997a).

ECOLOGICAL TAXONOMY OF INTELLECTUAL ASSESSMENT

Because assessment has veered too far in the direction of formal testing, and in light of these desiderata for new approaches to assessment, several researchers have proposed a more naturalistic, context sensitive, and valid ecological mode of assessment (Armour-Thomas & Gopaul-McNicol, in press; Ceci, 1990; Gardner, 1993). This is not a call to regress to a subjective form of evaluation. There is no reason to feel less confident about such a thorough approach because reliability can be achieved in these ecological approaches as well. In fact, these nonpsychometric measures that are based on multiple assessment instruments in multiple contexts have more ecological validity than psychometric measures that are based on a child's functioning in a controlled testing situation.

Another retort to the alleged objectivity of standardized formal tests is the fact that all tests are skewed toward a certain type of cognitive style. Thus, standardized tests are hostile to individuals who do not possess a blend of certain logical and linguistic intelligences and who are uncomfortable in decontextualized settings under impersonal and timed conditions. Correlatively, such tests are biased in favor of individuals who possess these strengths based on their prior cultural experiences.

Several researchers (Lave, 1977; Murtaugh, 1985; Rogoff, 1978) found that competency in using arithmetic operations in carrying out everyday duties is not always predictive on standardized arithmetic tests, although they tap the same arithmetic operations. For example, Carraher, Carraher, and Schlieman (1985) found that "street children" in Brazil intuitively developed models of probability to serve as street brokers for lottery tickets. Yet, these same children have difficulty applying these models to solve similar types of probability problems in educational settings. Moreover, the types of skills required for success on the Wechsler scales (Picture Arrangement and Similarities subtests) are similar to the deductive reasoning necessary in grocery shopping. Grocery shoppers tend to match prices comparing how similar or dissimilar items are, as well as plan whether the volume of their purchase can fit in their refrigerator. These examples confirm that there are instances where deficits in cognitive functioning disappear when the problem is couched in familiar terms or using familiar stimuli (Super, 1980). Therefore, cognition is indeed context sensitive and there exist multiple cognitive potentials instead of one cognitive potential or one central processor.

This ecological measure attempts to measure skills and behaviors that are relevant to the context in which a child lives (real-world type of intelligences, not just academic-type of intelligence). The child is assessed in several settings: the school, home, and community. Observing children's interaction with their family and friends in their most natural settings brings to the assessment robust knowledge of the family dynamics and cultural experiences of the child. The examiner should look for:

- The way children communicate.
- The way they socialize.
- The activities they engage in.
- The friendships they have.

- The roles they play.
- The respect or lack thereof they are given by family and friends.

In addition, the examiner assesses the child's intelligence by bringing some real-life experiences to the psychometric measure. For instance, if a child is unable to attain success on the Mazes subtest, take the child to a real-life maze situation and see if the child can find a way out. A child who cannot find a way out of a maze pictured on paper, but can maneuver out of a complex parking lot leaves us to wonder: Which environment more accurately tapped this individual's intelligence? Even intelligence experts such as Wechsler (1958) and Binet and Simon (1905) defined intelligence as one's ability to adapt to the real-world environment.

TEACHER QUESTIONNAIRE

What has been the child's previous educational experiences?

- Was the child ever retained?
- How often per week is the child absent?
- What has been the child's academic performance in:
    math—poor/fair/good/very good
    reading—poor/fair/good/very good
- Did the child participate in any supplemental instructional programs? If yes, what programs were they?
- What are the child's motivational/attention levels in class?
- How persistent is this child?
- How does the child relate to his/her peers?
- How does the child behave in class? In other words, is the child reflective or impulsive?
- Is the child responsible? How so?
- Is the child disciplined? How so?
- Does the child prefer to study alone or in a group?
- Does the child prefer dim or bright lights?

Based on the above findings, it is critical for clinicians to make recommendations commensurate with their assessment findings. Thus, if after doing potential *cognitive assessment*, the clinician should recommend what he/she believes are the best ways the teacher, parent, or mental health worker can intervene in working with the child. In other words, if *teaching* helped, then one should recommend one-on-one teaching for a particular number of sessions. If *extending time* helped, then one should recommend that the child be given extra time and more opportunity for practice. If *contextualizing* words helped, examiners should recommend that initially as the child acclimates to the new environment, he/she be given an opportunity to receive his/her assignment in a surrounding context. If the child was found to do better on *paper and pencil* tasks than on tasks requiring mental computations, then one should recommend that paper and pencil assessment be allowed. If the child has *other intelligences,* the examiner should recommend programs wherein these can be further enriched.

It is also important to use all of the *resources in the community*—church, social/recreational community programs, after school programs, legal aid, psychotherapeutic programs, etc.

In summary, a psychologist must be able to assist the school-based support team, the teacher, the family, and the child in developing a course of treatment that maximizes every opportunity for the child to move from his/her actual functioning to his/her potential functioning in a 3-year period. In other words, the child should show significant gains after the intervention period in all areas assessed (Armour-Thomas & Gopaul-McNicol, 1997a).

CONSIDERATION OF CULTURE IN REPORT WRITING

A CASE EXAMPLE

Presenting Problem and Client Description

Stephanie, a 12-year-old girl in sixth grade who was originally from Guyana, was referred for an initial evaluation by her teacher due to continued delays in all academic areas. The classroom teacher's records reflect that Stephanie was functioning on a third-grade level in math and a second-grade level in reading. The teacher felt that a special education program was needed to address Stephanie's academic delays.

The social history revealed that Stephanie lives with her mother, father, older sister, and grandmother. Her mother first came to the United States in the summer of 1994 and left her family in their homeland. The rest of the family, including Stephanie, followed two years later. All family members present themselves as a cohesive unit with strong extended family ties and good family support systems. According to Stephanie's parents, all developmental milestones were attained at age-expectant levels. However, there were reports of delays in reading upon her arrival in the United States. Her grandmother said that while "Stephanie was not a star in reading in Guyana, she was certainly able to read enough to get by. She is definitely not stupid as they are trying to say in school."

Behavioral Observation

Stephanie, a pleasant, warm, friendly girl, presented herself in a cooperative, compliant manner throughout all phases of the evaluation. In general, her response time was slow and she approached the testing in a cautious, reflective manner. When she clearly did not know the answer, she became noticeably embarrassed; she would lower her head, frown, and look away from the examiner. Anxiety was also noted: she would bite her nails and crack her knuckles. Confidence was clearly lacking on all of the psychometric verbal and nonverbal subtests. In contrast, Stephanie demonstrated more confidence when asked to perform similar tasks in her natural environment. Furthermore, the anxiety noted when presented with the psychometric tests was not evident in her ecology. Stephanie presented herself in a calm, relaxed, self-assured manner while she was doing the grocery shopping and other activities. The result revealed a positive increment in her overall performance when tested at home and in the community.

Psychometric Assessment

On the Wechsler Intelligence Scale for Children III (WISC-III), Stephanie obtained a full-scale IQ score that placed her in the moderate range of retardation in both the verbal and nonverbal areas (see Table 2.2). Individual subtests reveal moderate retardation in all areas assessed. Thus, on psychometric tests, Stephanie showed severe cognitive delays compared to her age-peers nationwide.

Psychometric Potential Assessment

Of note is that even when Stephanie was tested to her potential on the IQ test—for instance, when she was not placed under time pressure;

Table 2.2
Results of the Core Tests Administered

Wechsler Intelligence Scale for Children III

Psychometric Assessment	Range
Verbal Scale IQ	Moderate Retardation
Performance Scale IQ	Moderate Retardation
Full-Scale IQ	Moderate Retardation

Psychometric Potential Assessment	Range
Verbal Scale IQ	Deficient
Performance Scale IQ	Deficient
Full-Scale IQ	Deficient

Vineland Behavior Adaptive Scales–Parent Edition

	Range
Communication	Low
Social	Moderately Low
Daily Living Scales	Moderately Low

Other Intelligences

	Range
Musical Intelligence–Clarinet	Advanced
Bodily/Kinesthetic–Dance	Advanced

Ecological Assessment

	Range
Family/Community Support Assessment	Adequate

when item equivalencies as well as the test-teach-retest techniques were implemented; when the vocabulary words were contextually determined, that is, when asked to say the words in a surrounding context; or when time was suspended—deficiency in all areas was still evident (see Table 2.2). It was only when Stephanie was offered the opportunity to use paper and pencil that her cognitive functioning showed some significant gains. For instance, she clearly knew two-digit addition, subtraction, and multiplication, but had difficulty with one-digit division. Thus, by allowing Stephanie to use paper and pencil instead of relying on mental computations only, the examiner was able to determine that Stephanie had mastered some arithmetic skills but was unable to perform them without the aid of paper and pencil. In real-life situations, one is usually allowed the opportunity to work with pencil and paper, thus one can expect that Stephanie will be able to do basic calculations to function adequately well in her day-to-day duties.

Ecological Assessment

At home, in school, on the playground, and in the community, Stephanie is described as "bright, capable, and confident" by her family and friends. According to her mother, Stephanie prepares light lunches, helps with grocery shopping, and cares for her ailing grandmother when her mother is at work. In general, she performs all basic household and community chores commensurate to her age-peers.

Moreover, in observing Stephanie on the community playground, it was clearly evident that she was able to perform several of the tasks found on the IQ test. For instance, while she was unable to put the puzzles and blocks together on the Wechsler scales, she was adept at fixing a fan. Her mother explained that she fixes the appliances that malfunction at home. While assessing her ecologically, the examiner observed her as she dismantled the fan and reassembled it with no difficulty. Evidently, this activity involves the same visual-motor coordination skills as putting puzzles together. The fact that Stephanie was unable to reintegrate the pieces of puzzles on the IQ test, but assembled smaller, more complex parts of a fan, suggests that cultural factors must be impeding her ability to perform such a similar task on the standardized IQ test. Clearly, she is at least average in her visual-motor integration skills, albeit this was not evident on the psychometric measure.

Also significant was Stephanie's ability to remember a 13-item grocery list, although she was unable to recall as many as seven numbers on the Digit Span subtest of the Wechsler scales. Equally impressive was her ability to calculate basic addition and subtraction in the grocery store, although she demonstrated no mathematical concepts on the IQ test. Thus, in Stephanie's ecology, that is, in a real-life situation away from the testing environment, she showed good planning ability, good perceptual organization, fair mathematical skills, and good short-term memory. Unfortunately, none of these skills were manifested on the standardized, traditional IQ test, nor when she was tested to her cognitive potential via the same IQ measure. Evidently, from an ecological perspective, in real-life situations, Stephanie's cognitive ability is at least low average.

Other Intelligences Assessment

In spite of Stephanie's deficiencies in the verbal area on the IQ test, she was able to formulate melodic, rhythmic, and harmonic images into elaborate ideas after only one year of learning the clarinet (see Table 2.2). Furthermore, although she never studied the steelpan, she showed great affinity toward this instrument "after watching her uncle play for only three weeks." Her mother stated that she also has an interest in other musical instruments, such as the guitar and the flute. An interview with her music teacher revealed that Stephanie plays the clarinet with such fluency and composes music so creatively that in the realm of musical intelligence she would be considered superior intellectually.

An interview with Stephanie's gym teacher and the community sports teacher revealed that she was very athletic in most sports. She was said to have a well-developed sense of timing, coordination, and rhythm when these pertained to playing cricket and netball, and is "a star in dancing" (see Table 2.2). Her dance teacher says that she manifested accuracy, grace, speed, power, and great team spirit in all artistic endeavors. Also reported by her instructor was her ability to remain poised under pressure. An observation of her performing one of her dances allowed the examiner the opportunity to observe her bodily intelligence in its purest form, as she demonstrated flexibility and high technical proficiency.

Moreover, in observing her on the netball court, it was obvious that she had a well-developed sense of timing, coordination, and rhythm, which resulted in her being skillful in her gross and fine motor motions. Also of note was the social feedback offered by the sports teacher: "Stephanie is well respected by her peers, who often want her to play a leadership role in most competitions." She is described as "an inspiration to all." Thus, with respect to bodily/kinesthetic intelligence, she seems to be above average to superior.

Diagnostic Impression and Educational Implications

Intellectually, Stephanie is functioning in the moderate range of retardation on the WISC-III psychometric test and in the mentally deficient range on the psychometric potential assessment. Because Stephanie attended school in her native country on a regular basis, she cannot be said to be educationally deprived. A diagnosis of mental retardation cannot be given either, because only moderately low functioning was noted on the Vineland Adaptive Behavior Scales. To be diagnosed as mentally retarded, low functioning in social adaptation ought to be evident. Only on communication skills was she low, which was comparable to her score on the WISC-III psychometric test. After conducting a family assessment, it is clear that Stephanie functions adequately in her community and is respected by her peers. Thus, in spite of communication delays, there are no overall social adaptive deficiencies to characterize her as mentally retarded. At this juncture, Stephanie's intellectual functioning best fits the diagnosis of Leaning Disabled Not Otherwise Specified. This category is for learning disorders that do not meet the criteria for any specific learning disorder and may include problems in all three core areas of reading, mathematics, and written expression.

Given the obvious delays in all academic skill areas and on the psychometric IQ test, one would be inclined to provide Stephanie with intensive instruction in all academic cognitive skill areas on a daily basis in a small, special educational classroom setting. Clearly, she does require the supportive environment of supplemental instruction. However, given her performance when assessed in other settings beyond the IQ testing environment, a less restrictive setting outside of the special education self-contained realm ought to be explored. For instance, Stephanie should be encouraged to pursue music, in particular the clarinet. Likewise, she ought to be encouraged to perfect her athletic skills, given her intellectual prowess in these areas as well. As such, the typical special education self-contained class where there is little emphasis on honing one's career or occupational skills is not recommended.

Stephanie's obvious intelligence in music renders her a prime candidate for a scholarship at a music school. Opportunities for career-related academic skill development, including essential work adjustment skills and direct work experience through daily practice in a music school, are needed for this child to attain her potential and be self-supportive.

Recommendations

The recommendations for Stephanie included a referral to Operation Athlete, an organization in New York City that provides scholarships for gifted athletes. This organization has an afterschool program whose goal is to recruit intelligent athletes who can go on to become professionals in their areas of expertise. Stephanie was recently offered a scholarship for remedial aid in all academic areas. According to school officials, if she remains motivated and shows great effort, other scholarships, even a possible college scholarship (depending on her academic performance) is guaranteed. Stephanie was also referred to Sesame Flyer, a Caribbean organization that teaches immigrant families to play the steelpan, the guitar, and other musical instruments.

A follow-up on Stephanie's progress one year after the completion of the evaluation revealed a continued superiority in the nonacademic tasks, such as sports, and a slight positive increment in the academic areas. Stephanie was taught to transfer her knowledge from her ecology to the classroom setting by various exercises offered by the examiner, who continued treatment following the evaluation. Teacher and family consultation to assist those who work more closely with Stephanie was offered on an ongoing basis. The most recent teacher report revealed "significant gains in math, vocabulary, and spelling." Stephanie ought to be monitored closely and assessed every six months to determine if a less restrictive environment should be provided.

CONCLUSION

Assessment programs that fail to take into account the differences among individuals' cultural experiences are anachronistic. To take these variations into account would require those in the formal testing enterprise to suspend some of the major assumptions of standardized testing, such as uniformity of individuals' experiences and the penchant for one type of cost-efficient instrument. Psychologists in training should be taught about individual differences by being introduced formally to such distinctions because it is difficult for students in training to arrive at such empirically valid taxonomies of differences in individuals on

their own. Such exposure should occur during their professional training. Once exposed to different profiles in the course of their apprentice-
ships, it is easier for them to be more flexible in their assessment
practices. Likewise, it is equally important for students to be cognizant
of individual state regulations regarding bilingual and bicultural assessment; in several states, there are chancellor's disclaimant statements for assessing bilingual children. The reader should refer to Table
2.1, which presents a summary of the stages of the bio-ecological assessment report.

In summary, the most critical dimension to assessment is getting at
the strengths of a child and helping that child to feel a sense of empowerment and success in spite of any obvious academic deficiency
(Gopaul-McNicol & Armour-Thomas, 1997b).

CHAPTER 3

Assessment of Cross-Cultural Parenting

T HIS CHAPTER IS focused on the assessment of parenting skills across cultures. The underlying philosophy of this section is that first, therapists must utilize their entire repertoire of skills (pencil and paper tests, clinical interviewing, projective tests, role playing, behavioral observation, etc.) to make a thorough evaluation. Second, therapists must extend the boundaries of what has up until now typically been considered the areas germane to the explanation of parenting. The topic of parenting will be discussed in terms of cultural norms, the advantages and disadvantages of formal assessment scales, the impact of immigration, the impact of ethnic identity, the impact of racism, discipline, medical care, and education.

CULTURAL NORMS

Sue and Sue (1990) talk about the importance of considering the worldview of the client and the worldview of the therapist. Differences in their views can strongly influence the therapeutic relationship and hence the outcome of treatment: "world views are not only composed of our attitudes, values, opinions and concepts, but also they may affect how we think, make decisions, behave, and define events" (Sue & Sue, 1990, p. 137).

It is natural, then, to assume that the worldview of a particular family will shape the adults in that family, particularly ideas and decisions regarding the parenting of children. Although knowledge about a family's cultural group membership (e.g., Asian, Black, Spanish, Australian, etc.) is helpful, it does not mean that there is necessarily a blanket worldview held by all members of that group.

An often overlooked aspect of parenting evaluations is the contribution of cultural norms regarding child care and child rearing (Canino & Spurlock, 1994). We have placed the issues of inquiry into the following clusters:

1. *Conception, pregnancy, and delivery.* When are women expected to start raising families? How is birth control viewed? What type of prenatal care is expected or usual? Is there a preferred method of childbirth? How involved do they want members of the medical establishment to be? Are there other people in the community who deliver babies? How involved is the father in the birth process? How is the pregnancy viewed: as something to be ashamed of and hidden or as something to be proud of? Are women considered "ill" at this time, or is pregnancy seen as a natural life process?

2. *Infant care.* Who takes primary responsibility for care of the infant? What are the attitudes about breast feeding versus bottle feeding, sleeping patterns, feeding patterns, and so on? How are crying spells dealt with and what meaning is attributed to them?

3. *The older child.* What are the attitudes about child care? What are the attitudes about education? Are there preferences for a particular sex? What are the expectations for boys? What are the expectations for girls? Who are the important people in the child's life?

4. *Discipline.* What are the attitudes about discipline (examined in more detail in Chapter 5)?

5. *Nature of relationships.* Are parent-child relationships seen as hierarchical or democratic and equal? What do the parents see as their obligations to their children? What are the children's obligations to their parents?

6. *Young adults.* How is success defined for the young girl? How is success defined for the young boy? Are young adults expected to leave home? If so, when? If so, under what conditions?

7. *Health care.* How do parents decide when it is appropriate to seek medical care for their children? How do they carry out physician

instructions? Are the parents attentive to cues from their children that may be indicative of illness? Is any preventive health care done?

ASSESSMENT OF PARENTING SKILLS

There have been a few formal instruments designed to assess parenting abilities. One such instrument is the Perception of Parental Role Scales developed by Lucia Gilbert and Gary Hanson in 1982. The purpose of the instrument is to measure the parent's perceived role responsibilities. The test yields scores in the following three areas: (a) teaching the child (norms, social values, personal hygiene, physical health, survival, cognitive development, social skills, and handling emotions); (b) meeting the basic and emotional needs of the child; and (c) the interface of family and society (Murphy, Conoley, & Impara, 1994).

Another scale is the Parenting Stress Index, third edition, developed by Richard Abidin in 1983. The target population is parents of children age 12 and older. Abidin intended the scale to be used to identify stressors related to dysfunctional parenting. This test yields scores in the following three areas: (a) the child domain (adaptability, acceptability, demandingness, mood, hyperactivity, distractibility, and reinforces parent); (b) the parent domain (depression, attachment, restrictions of role, sense of competence, social isolation, relationship with spouse, and parental health); and (c) an overall life stress score (Murphy et al., 1994).

The Parent Behavior Checklist was published in 1994 and developed by Robert Fox. This scale was intended for use with parents of children between the ages of 1 and 4. The scores are in the areas of expectations, discipline, and nurturing (Murphy et al., 1994).

There are several advantages and disadvantages to the use of these tests. On the positive side, they are self-administered, do not take long to complete, and are easy to score. One major disadvantage when considering cultural diversity and the possibility of language problems is the heavy reliance on the parent's reading and comprehension abilities. Another problem has to do with how well these scales include issues germane to the raising of children in certain cultures (e.g., how to raise children to maintain their practice of the Jewish faith when the majority of their classmates are Christian; how to raise children of color to be proud of their appearance).

In the absence of a wider selection of parenting scales, we make the following recommendations to assist in assessment. Direct observation of parent-child interactions can yield very useful information, and this can be accomplished in a variety of ways. Parents can be left in a play-room that has a one-way mirror and instructed to simply play with their children. The same kind of naturalistic observation can go on during home visits. These situations allow the therapist to see how the parent attempts to engage the child, how the parent handles rejection from the child, how much autonomy the parent allows the child to have, how the parent defines play, how the parent handles the child's full range of emotions (happiness, sadness, anger, fear, etc.), how the parent teaches rules, and how the parent handles misbehavior. From a cultural viewpoint, these situations may help therapists to understand how parents define good behavior and bad behavior in their children. The therapist may also learn if the parents have any culture-specific ways of explaining their children's behavior.

Role plays provide another opportunity for direct observation of parenting style. Parents and children can be given a slip of paper describing an incident for them to act out. Also, incidents can be solicited from members of the family; for example, parents and children can relate to the therapist what actually happened at home and then use the role play to depict how they ideally would have liked things to turn out.

An additional source of information about parents can come from other people. Extended family members, teachers, guidance counselors, and pediatricians are just a few of the sources. However, the therapist must always consider the information from an individual within the larger context of other information gathered.

Projective techniques have enormous potential for use with culturally diverse populations. The development of the Tell-Me-A-Story test is proof of this. One of the major problems with projective tests, however, is the use of stimulus material that lacks relevancy for members of cultures that are not mainstream. For example, in one case, a storyboard made up of pictures of people was shown to a Korean child, but none of the people depicted remotely resembled an Asian person. To remedy some of these problems, Landgarten (1993) developed the Magazine Photo Collage Technique. This is not a prepackaged test, as the stimulus "cards" are provided by the therapist. The first step in gathering this material is to cut pictures out of magazines. The pictures fall into two categories: miscellaneous pictures and people pictures. The following is Landgarten's list of what the people photos should include:

1. A variety of persons from different cultures. The largest number should pertain to the client's population.
2. The vast majority should be reality oriented, with only a few stereotyped glamorous pictures.
3. Male and female figures.
4. Persons of all ages.
5. A variety of facial expressions.
6. Movement and static body positions.
7. Varied economic conditions that display different walks of life.
8. Individuals placed in different types of environment.
9. Individuals who stand alone, are in dyads, are part of a group, or are in a family setting (p. 5).

When used for the purposes of assessment, the following instructions are given to the client. First, the client is asked to reach into the box containing the miscellaneous pictures and choose eye-catching ones. The client is then asked to free-associate with the chosen pictures. Next, the client is told to choose five or six people from the people photos, paste them onto paper, and indicate what each person is thinking. In the third task, the client has access to both boxes of photos. He or she is asked to pick photos that symbolize something "good" and photos that symbolize something "bad." The final task involves choosing one picture from the people box and pasting it to a piece of paper. The client is asked three questions. What is happening to that person? Do you think that person's situation will change? and What will make the situation change (Landgarten, 1993)?

The first task can provide the therapist with some idea about what might be of primary concern to the client at the moment, and the second task gets at the discrepancy between what is said and what is thought; this could be enormously helpful with some Asian clients for whom a separation of thought and word is important and who maintain a public persona. The final task can supply information about problem-solving skills, coping mechanisms, and defensive structure.

One of the drawbacks of this technique when used for assessment purposes is that there is no uniformity across clients. In other words, clients from different cultures will be presented with boxes of different stimulus photos. Clients from the same culture may get the same box of stimulus photos, but they will pick different photos from the boxes. This makes it difficult to standardize the "instrument" and make any intragroup or intergroup comparisons.

IMPACT OF IMMIGRATION ON PARENTING

It has been said that parenting has probably never been as difficult and complicated as it is in today's society. For some immigrants, a big contributor to the complexity of the parenting task is the immigration experience. The trip to America—how it was planned or not planned, the reasons for it, and how it was made—has the potential to alter family structure and disrupt the family life cycle.

Sometimes, when the decision to immigrate is made and appropriate papers secured, not all family members are able to make the trip at once. The person or persons able to work are the ones who make the trip first. This necessitates leaving minor children behind. Some parents may feel that they are unable to act in their capacity as parents because they are miles away and do not have a direct hand in the day-to-day life of the child. Extended family members (grandparents, aunts and uncles, older cousins) may serve as surrogate parents (Brice-Baker, 1996). Older siblings may become "parentified" as they seek to fill a real or imagined void left by the parents.

Although there are very real limitations to long-distance parenting, a useful part of any parenting assessment with immigrant families is a discussion about how the separation between parent and child was handled. Does the parent show some awareness of the impact of his or her extended absence on the child? Did the parent give an age-appropriate explanation of the reason for and the length of time of the separation? Is there a way that the surrogate caregiver can get in touch with the parent about major decisions concerning the child? What is the child's understanding about family reunification? How has communication been maintained (phone calls, letters, pictures, etc.; Brice-Baker, 1996)?

When children are brought to the United States and live with their parents, the reunion is not without its problems. Parents may infantalize children, who were young at the point of the initial separation, ignoring the intervening months or years. These parents may need help letting go and mourning what they missed in their child's development. They need to meet the child at his or her current stage. Children may not recognize their parents as the nuclear family executives. This is a particularly strong issue in those cultures where family structure is hierarchical and generational boundaries are quite rigid. It is important for the therapist to understand how the parent handles the child's acts of rebellion and what meaning the parent assigns to that behavior.

The timing of family reunification and its impact on the life cycle stages of the family should be assessed. Adolescents, who are attempting to establish their own identities and need a certain amount of space to accomplish this, might struggle against a parent's effort to promote togetherness. In a similar vein, immigrant parents looking forward to and needing some fairly self-reliant children may find themselves surprised when a child shows signs of regression. In addition to assessing the aspects of parenting mentioned in the preceding sections of this chapter, it could be useful for a therapist to also assess parental expectations. In fact, a revealing exercise in therapeutic sessions is for therapists to elicit the expectations of each parent and each child and then look at the extent to which there is agreement between parents (within the executive subsystem) and between generations.

Even when families do not immigrate in a fragmented fashion, but instead as a whole, there is a potential for many challenges to parenting abilities. One challenge has to do with the inversion of the generational hierarchy. This can come about when children have mastery of English and/or greater familiarity with the American culture (Brice-Baker, 1996). The exposure to English in the school system gives children a distinct advantage over their parents. When they leave their homes and interact with authority figures outside of their own culture, it is the children who often act as translators for adults. The role of translator gives them power they would not ordinarily have. In some cases, it makes them privy to "adult talk confidences," thereby crossing a boundary that in some cultures is important to maintain.

Another challenge can come from children's thinking that their parents are "too ethnic" or "too strict" (Gopaul-McNicol, 1993). For these children, the term *too ethnic* refers to the range of behaviors their parents engage in that make the extent of their differences evident to their peers. The descriptor *too strict* for immigrant children differs from mainstream children since the parents of a typical adolescent immigrant child expect their child to give them a detailed breakdown as to what they do when they are away from the home; in other words, little liberty is accorded such children unlike their American counterparts who are permitted to be assertive and even make decisions independently—a rather positive attribute for them, but a negative one for immigrant children. Reactions to parental authority can range from embarrassment to acting-out behavior. Therapists will find it useful to assess the differing levels of acculturation on the part of different family members. How understanding are the parents of a child's need to be accepted and fit in with the majority? Are the parents able to exercise differential flexibility with regard to their child's attempts to move away from the old cultural ways, or do they maintain the same position regardless of the issue? Parents should be aware of their own cultural values regarding discipline and be able to pinpoint the areas of convergence and divergence. A plan should be formulated to deal with the child's confusion about information coming from multiple sources (what their parents tell them is appropriate behavior, what their teachers tell them is normal or appropriate behavior, and what they observe or are allowed to do in the homes of their American friends). In some cultures, a child's seeming misbehavior is viewed as a sign of ungratefulness after the sacrifices the parents and extended family members have made to make things better.

Another concern is that of the chronological age of the child upon re-entry into the family; many children join their parents in their adolescent years which can be a particular vulnerable time. Besides, just when parents may be beginning to solidify relationships with their children, they are faced with losing them to college, marriage, or a new job. They may be reluctant to let go, desiring more time together. Some children at this stage may actually be hesitant about moving on, unsure about their parents' or younger siblings' ability to cope, and anxious about their own ability to achieve.

THE IMPACT OF ETHNIC IDENTITY ON PARENTING

A significant part of a parent's job is to help children develop a stable and secure identity. It is incumbent upon therapists, as part of an assessment of parenting skills, to determine how parents are accomplishing this task. Bernal and Knight (1993) define *ethnic identity* as how one sees oneself within the context of one's ethnic group. Isajiw (1990) breaks this concept into two parts: external ethnic identity and internal ethnic identity. They are defined as follows:

External ethnic identity—refers to observable social and cultural behaviors

Internal ethnic identity—has three dimensions: cognitive, moral, and affective. The cognitive dimension refers to the ethnic person's (a) self images and images of his or her ethnic group, (b) knowledge of the ethnic group's heritage and its historical past, and (c) knowledge of the ethnic group's values. The moral dimension . . . refers to the ethnic person's feelings of group obligations . . . the affective refers to an ethnic person's feelings of attachment to his or her own ethnic group. (Isajiw, 1990, cited in Sodowsky, Kwan, & Pannu, 1995 p. 138)

Although a great deal of work in multicultural assessment has been done on the concept of ethnic identity, the thrust of that work has been on the creation of models that can adequately describe the stage of development (Suzuki, Meller, & Ponterotto, 1996). There is no instrument to give parents that will tell how they might be helping or impeding this development. It should be noted that we are not advocating the assessment of parents' roles in ethnic identity development of their children in order to assign blame or in any way to suggest that their children need to be, for example, "more Italian," or "more Polish." This assessment should have following goals:

1. Determining how important ethnic identification is to the parents.
2. Determining how parents might feel thwarted in their efforts to pass on a cultural legacy to their children.
3. Identifying strengths in the parents that could have been overlooked.

One method of gathering information pertinent to Isajiw's (1990) external ethnic identity is through a clinical interview. In such an interview, the therapist can find out how culture is transmitted to the child. For example, the therapist can learn whether a language other than English is spoken in the home and if ethnic clothes are worn at home. In many families, it is not uncommon for the parents to go to work in "American" business suits and skirts and blouses, but, when they return home, participate in activities in the neighborhood, or attend their house of worship, they don more ethnic attire.

Another way culture is transmitted is through food. Children grow up eating foods at home that their classmates are unfamiliar with. Daughters may be taught by their mothers how to prepare specific dishes. American food may be eaten only when family members are away from home. There may be special foods for special occasions. Teaching children about ethnic food and its preparation is not just about passing along family recipes. Some ethnic groups have dietary laws that dictate which foods can be eaten. Special meaning may be assigned to certain foods, and how one eats may be important. Participating in a meal with the rest of the family may be more significant for some groups than observing holidays together.

A highly visible way of communicating culture is through the home environment. How have the parents chosen to decorate their home? There may be ethnic fabrics used in the decor. There may be knick-knacks scattered about the house that pertain to specific ethnic historical figures or events. The pictures on the walls may reflect the family's ethnicity.

Rituals are often so automatic that parents may not realize what message their performance is giving. A therapist can ask about important religious or secular holidays, if they are celebrated, and how. Sometimes people are not even aware that a particular custom is just something that people in their culture do. One way of obtaining this information is to ask open-ended questions about unusual life cycle events, for example, What happens or what is done when a baby is born? How is a marriage celebrated?

An important job parents have is providing cultural role models for their children. What kinds of groups or organizations does the family belong to? Are the children provided with opportunities to hear about, see, meet, or interact with people of their culture who are successful?

And finally, how is the parent handling the negative information the child may hear on the evening news, at a friend's house, in school, and elsewhere? Does the parent talk to the child about ethnic stereotypes? Are ethnic stereotypes used in the home? Does the parent answer the child's questions after the child has heard a derogatory comment about a member of their ethnic group? Does the parent ignore the query and hope the child forgets? Does the parent send the child to someone else for an explanation?

Not all of the information mentioned above can or should be gathered in an interview format. In fact, some of the items can be more accurately observed in a home visit. The tremendous drawbacks of home visits on the already overworked therapist have been duly noted. For example, time is needed to travel to and from the clients' home as well as time for the session. There may be interruptions, making for a less than ideal therapeutic meeting. However, home visits do have tremendous value for families who have been marginalized by mainstream society. They get an opportunity to meet with the therapist on their own turf, which can encourage an increased level of comfort. The therapist's willingness to make the trip can be seen as an example of the therapist's flexibility. From the therapist's point of view there are benefits as well: the therapist gets a chance to observe the family in a naturalistic setting; seeing what is important to this family by observing their environment.

DISCIPLINE

The issue of discipline is a very sensitive topic in psychotherapy. Parents and guardians of children who come from cultures that have been marginalized in our society have come to expect blame and criticism about the way they handle their children—and more specifically, how they discipline their children. That therapists are charged with the duty of reporting cases of alleged child abuse and neglect has seriously altered our roles. Instead of functioning as therapists, we become enforcers of the law. Instead of being accepting, we become judgmental.

One of the problems in cross-cultural assessment and treatment is the indiscriminant use of mainstream standards to judge clients who are not part of the mainstream. There is a paucity of research on parenting and discipline practices in different cultures. Payne (1989) did such a study in the West Indies. The subjects were adult members of the general population. However, people who worked with children in a professional capacity (e.g., teachers) were excluded from the sample. The purpose of the study was to determine attitudes toward corporal punishment. The results indicated that hitting children with a belt was approved of by three-fourths of the sample. The strengths of this study lie in the fact that the research looked at one culture (Barbadians); that the specific issue of corporal punishment was raised instead of some euphemism; that specific subcategories of corporal punishment were inquired about (i.e., what is used in hitting: hand, belt; where on the body the child is hit); and that people's reasoning behind their endorsement of corporal punishment was ascertained. We are not endorsing corporal punishment. However, we are suggesting the need for more studies like Payne's. In cases where discipline crosses the line into abuse, it is important that therapists have a better understanding of what happened.

Another issue in cross-cultural therapeutic dyads and perceptions of disciplinary practices in different cultures is the part played by the acceptance of myths and stereotypes by therapists. One example of this is the very common belief that only people of color hit their children. Turner (1994) discusses the unconscious need for White society in antebellum times to perceive and depict Black men and women as violent. It has been eye-opening in our experience doing supervision of White trainees how many times abuse and neglect are suspected in Black families when similar behavior in White families is ignored.

We have found the following practices to be helpful in our assessment of discipline:

1. How do the parents define discipline, and what do they see as the purpose of discipline?
2. Do the parents see any difference between discipline and punishment?
3. What forms of discipline do they use?
4. If corporal punishment is used, is it used across the board or only for certain behaviors?
5. How is it decided that corporal punishment is appropriate for the particular behavior mentioned in number 4?
6. Is anyone else allowed to discipline the child? If yes, who?
7. Do the parents believe in the concept of the incorrigible child?
8. If they believe in the concept of incorrigibility, how is it dealt with?
9. What responsibility, if any, do they believe parents have for a child's behavior?
10. If the parents are immigrants, what knowledge do they have of the child protective laws in this country?

11. Are there certain aspects of being a member of their culture that make it imperative to discipline their children about certain things other parents do not have to worry about?
12. What role does spirituality play in their disciplinary practices?
13. Who, within the family structure, is considered the appropriate person to decide on and mete out punishment for children?
14. Are there any cultural explanations for why a child misbehaves?

MEDICAL CARE

An important aspect of parenting is giving attention to health problems a child has and taking steps to prevent illness. Therapists will find it useful to examine the intersection of culture and social class and how these variables singly and together may impact upon parents' ability to accomplish their duties. "Economically disadvantaged minority families often lack good health maintenance care" (Canino & Spurlock, 1994, p. 29). The adults in these families may lack employment and therefore not have the funds for visits to the pediatrician. Some family members hold jobs that do not offer health insurance. In cases where health insurance is available, families may not be able to afford the copayment. Many economically strapped adults turn to pediatric clinics in area hospitals. The reality of trying to get care in these clinics is disheartening. Often due to staff shortages, parents can get appointments for their children only far into the future. They see a different pediatrician at each visit, disrupting the continuity of care. Once there, the wait for service is long. This can be a major issue for parents who may hold jobs where they clock in and are liable to lose pay for any time they are absent. Once the doctor is seen, parents may wait again at the clinic pharmacy to have prescriptions filled.

Any one of these barriers to treatment or a combination of them can place economically disadvantaged parents in the position of going for medical care only when it is absolutely necessary. This also leads to a reliance on hospital emergency rooms for routine or well-baby visits. When financial resources are limited or nonexistent, it is important for therapists not to frame parents' behavior in a pejorative way.

Immigration status can also influence the way a parent functions regarding his or her child's health care. Few countries outside of the United States have the extensive and advanced medical services available here. There may be some immigrants coming from tropical climates who are unfamiliar with the way to dress a young child in cold weather. The idea of prophylactic medicine may be foreign to immigrant parents. They may not be aware of vaccinations available here for childhood diseases (measles, mumps, diphtheria, etc.) that we take for granted. And, in cases where people are aware of these things, the access to certain types of treatment may be even more restricted in their respective countries than they are here.

Once finances and immigration status are taken into consideration, one can examine how culture has shaped parents' attitudes about medical treatment. We have found it useful in our practices to find out:

1. What experience the parents have with physicians.
2. What folk remedies or mythology exists about certain illnesses.
3. Whether they seek the help of folk healers.
4. If and when they go to doctors, what their expectations are.
5. If there is any particular mindset about taking pills.
6. What type of preventive medicine is practiced.
7. What their fears are about taking their child to the doctor.

In some cultures, the mind, body, and spirit are not viewed as separate entities. As such, there may be more of a focus on healing the spirit of a child than mending his or her body. In some people's belief system, medicine is to be taken only after symptoms have presented themselves. This is contrary to the notion of prophylactic medicine, taken to prevent the onset of illness.

EDUCATION

The job of parenting includes seeing to the educational needs of one's children. The manner in which parents perform this job can be influenced by cultural attitudes regarding formal education, socioeconomic status, immigration status, and level of acculturation among others.

Therapists may encounter differences in parental attitudes and expectations regarding their children's academic performance. In some cultures, education is highly regarded and may be part of the definition of personal success; for these parents, children's getting top grades, going to Ivy League colleges, pursuing graduate degrees, and entering certain professions may be of the utmost importance. In other cultures, education may be less important; the emphasis may be less on how much money their children end up earning or the status accorded their profession by society and more on the integrity of the line of work they choose, the reliability of employment opportunities, a regular paycheck, and the ability to support oneself and one's family. There is also the issue of how education is defined by the parents. When many of us in American society refer to education, we are referring to formal schooling. Some cultures place equal or more emphasis on a child's spiritual and moral education, a child's education regarding family obligations, or a child's education in a particular trade (house building, farming, etc.). It should be noted that there are no absolutes in this area, and the level of acculturation certainly competes with the impact of some of these cultural influences.

Not all of the factors influencing the course of a child's education are controlled by the parents. Limited financial resources and residence in low-income neighborhoods restrict access to better schools. There is often no money for tutoring (if needed) or to take advantage of educational enrichment opportunities. Rigid work schedules may make the supervision of homework difficult. Parents with limited finances may feel powerless to advocate for their child within the school system.

As was mentioned earlier, differences in immigration status and level of acculturation have their effects too. Parents who lack fluency in English may be embarrassed to speak to school officials and may be overwhelmed by the school system. Parents coming from other countries may be mystified as to the appropriate grade their child should be placed in. They may lack familiarity with child study teams and intelligence and academic testing procedures. In some cases, parents may not be cognizant of their right to question academic decisions made by the school or their right to see reports on their child and have them explained (Gopaul-McNicol, 1993). "Normal but underachieving minority students whose language at home differs from that used in school are often overrepresented in programs for the learning disabled" (Ortiz & Yates, 1983, cited in Canino & Spurlock, 1994, p. 21). Parents struggling with English language fluency themselves may not know how to help their children or grasp the consequences of being labeled.

CHAPTER 4

Assessment of Intermarried Couples

T HE ISSUES OF culture can play an interesting part in the therapeutic work that we do with couples. The most obvious way
psychotherapists may confront these issues is in their work
with interracial, interreligious, or interethnic couples. When the partners present themselves for treatment, there is a strong likelihood that
finding common ground in disparate backgrounds may either contribute to their problems or strengthen their relationship. Differences
do not always make for conflict. Oftentimes, when people are presum-
ably very different, more of an effort is made to avoid assumptions
and seek understanding.

In an alternative scenario, therapists from one culture may find themselves working with couples in which both partners share the same culture. This is not unlike individual therapeutic situations in which the
therapist is culturally dissimilar from the patient. There may be a lack of
understanding, on the part of the therapist, of the couples' cultural or religious framework. To make matters even more complex, the spouses
may be members of the same cultural and religious groups but reflect
some of the diversity within that group. For example, a Black couple
may present for treatment. The husband could be from the northern
United States and his wife from the southern United States. This union
reflects regional differences. In another example, a therapist could treat
a Black couple in which the husband was originally from Jamaica and
the wife was born and raised in the United States. They are both Black,

but they come from different countries. In both of these cases one might grossly simplify things by talking about a Black culture and miss the subtleties of the other differences.

In yet another scenario, couples work has the potential to expand into family work, and therapists may work with children and adolescents who are the products of an intermarriage. Some of the work in these families could involve the development of an identity for the child, dealing with the fallout from assigning positive or negative traits to each parent's respective culture or religion, feelings associated with being forced to choose to identify with one race or another (or one religion or another), and so on.

While there is certainly a degree of overlap among these scenarios, this chapter will primarily focus on the first clinical situation: doing assessments with intermarried couples.

CLARIFICATION OF TERMS

Baptiste (1984) defines *intermarriage* as a marriage wherein one spouse's racial, cultural, and/or religious background is or was different from the other's (p. 373). Suzuki and Kugler (1995) define *assessment* as a process through which a clinician obtains information about a client. The assessment process includes both quantitative and qualitative information that can be put together to provide a more comprehensive picture of the total functioning of a client (p. 493). In keeping with these definitions, the authors will highlight some of the qualitative data that can be helpful to the therapist's understanding of the intermarried couple. We will also discuss the applicability of some of the existing formal assessment devices.

AREAS OF ASSESSMENT

THE PROBLEM

This phase of the assessment process provides useful information and can be a springboard for establishing a therapeutic working alliance with the couple. How did the couple get to the therapist's office? In other words, are they self-referred, and if not, who did refer them? This question has been asked in culturally similar couples; however, it can take on a new meaning for the spouse who comes from a culture or religion that does not look favorably upon psychotherapy or the particular referral source.

Take as an example the case of Mr. and Mrs. Boule, an interracial couple. François Boule, a native Haitian, immigrated to the United States as a young adult. His wife, Jean, was a young, White, French Catholic woman he met while they were both in graduate school. They have a 10-year-old son. The school authorities repeatedly charged Mr. Boule with the physical abuse of his son. When he failed to respond to their demands for meetings with the guidance counselors, teachers, and principal of the school, they finally contacted the authorities with their suspicions. After an initial investigation of this alleged abuse, Mr. and Mrs. Boule were referred for therapy. Mr. Boule was outraged. From his perspective, there was no abuse. He was simply disciplining his son, as was his right. However, in addition to his outrage about the accusation, he could not understand how, as he saw it, the government (in the form of child protective services) could interfere with a father's decision making regarding his family. In his native Haiti, the government, at times, had done many terrible things, but interfering in a father's discipline of his child was not one of them.

In the above illustration, it is helpful to assess what each spouse's feelings are about the referral process and their respective understanding of the ramifications, if any, of not complying with a therapy recommendation or mandate. For some individuals, particularly immigrants coming from police states, the idea of free will is nonexistent. They may be overly compliant out of fear. Others may be undercompliant out of a lack of experience in their own countries with helpful governmental agencies. Therapists can gain more ground with a couple if they separate the two issues of motivation for treatment and feelings of dyscontrol.

Another area of inquiry for the therapist is each spouse's definition of the problem. If there is no congruence about the definition of the problem, it is then important to know if it is a result of their cultural differences. McGoldrick, Pearce, and Giordano (1982) point out that knowledge about cultural values informs a therapist about what is seen as a problem, determines when someone goes for help, determines whom they go to for help, and what they expect from that person. Knowledge about the culture also gives general information regarding attitudes about mental illness and psychotherapy. In intermarriage, there may be differences about whether or not there is a problem as well as different interpretations of the behavior considered to be a problem.

Case Example

Olympia was a 24-year-old Italian American woman. She was born in southern Italy and lived there until the age of 15, when she came to the United States. She came to treatment complaining of a variety of anxiety symptoms. The therapist explored various aspects of her life, including the relationship with her boyfriend. According to Olympia, Carl was uncaring and she harbored fears that their relationship was doomed. The therapist and Olympia determined that her concerns about this relationship were of sufficient magnitude to warrant inviting Carl in for some couples sessions. Carl agreed to participate in therapy, although he saw this only as an opportunity to help Olympia. He did not believe that he needed any therapy and in fact informed the therapist that he did not really believe in it. When he showed up, some preliminary demographic information was gathered. It was learned that Carl was a 27-year-old White male of German background. Olympia described in detail what she thought the problem was, namely, the absence of any physical displays of affection, his cold and calculating responses to her everyday concerns, and his upset over her crying spells. Carl, who did not believe that there were any problems in the relationship, or elsewhere for that matter, proceeded to respond to Olympia's concerns. Carl related to the therapist that he had always been someone who valued problem solving. He thought that Olympia's crying spells and hysteria were a waste of time. He saw little to gain in focusing on affect. He described himself and his family as pragmatists, and he proudly attributed that trait to his German heritage. After listening to Carl, Olympia began to discuss her southern Italian heritage. She said that the degree of one's concern and caring was measured by rather passionate shows of affection, anger, grief, and so on. Olympia said that it was difficult for her to proceed to any problem solving until she got all her feelings out.

Although there are certainly culturally homogeneous couples who present with similar issues, there are some key issues particular to the intermarried couple. First, the cultural lens that each partner brought to the relationship put an entirely different interpretation on Carl's behavior. Second, the cultural differences between them could be used therapeutically to diffuse a lot of anger and make things seem less personal. In other words, if Olympia could see Carl's behavior in the broader context of his cultural heritage, it would make his actions seem less deliberate, personalized, and intractable. The same could be said for Carl's view of Olympia's behavior. And finally, it is helpful to keep in mind that cultural values determine what one labels a problem. In this case, Carl was cognizant of his own behavior and Olympia's; however, his failure to be emotionally expressive was not seen as a problem by him.

CULTURAL NORMS

Before a therapist can interpret whether or to what degree culture plays a role in orchestrating a couple's interactions, the therapist should have a sense of the areas of cultural overlap as well as the areas of cultural disparity. One way of accomplishing this is by gaining knowledge about what is expected of husbands and wives in their respective cultures. The following items are suggested areas of inquiry (they are not necessarily meant to serve as part of a structured interview).

1. What is the normative age for men and women at the time of marriage?
2. Why is it that most people tend to marry at that age?
3. When is a man considered eligible for marriage? Does he have to accomplish certain things or simply attain a certain age?
4. When is a woman considered eligible for marriage?
5. To what degree are marriages a matter of free will?
6. Is there a history of arranged marriages?
7. If so, whose job is it to make such arrangements?
8. When people in this particular culture immigrate to other countries, does the custom of arranging marriages continue?
9. If marriages are not arranged, what is the basis for mate selection?
10. To what extent are mutual attraction, common interests, and love a part of the decision-making process?
11. What are the expected duties of a husband?
12. What are the expected duties of a wife?
13. To what extent do the gender roles enumerated above adhere to patriarchal norms?
14. What is the division of power expected to be in the relationship?
15. What happens when the power equation is altered?

16. What are the attitudes toward premarital sex for men and for women?

17. What are the attitudes about extramarital affairs for men and for women?

18. Are there certain norms for sexual behavior within marriage?

Answers to the above can be ascertained through formal questioning of the couple during sessions or through the use of questionnaires that the couple can take home. The therapist can gain helpful information from reading works on the sociology of family life, on attitudes about work, on historical accounts of immigrant experiences, on the role of religion, and so on. However, one must be careful to avoid stereotyping and be open to the heterogeneity within each culture. One way to gather the above material and create an opportunity for joining with the couple is to bring in articles one has read about each spouse's culture and ask for their respective opinions. This activity makes the spouses active participants and demonstrates the therapist's willingness to learn about them rather than make assumptions.

EXPECTATIONS

The next area of assessment involves weighing what the therapist knows about the cultural norms against the expectations of each partner. Every couple the authors have seen in clinical practice, whether they were intermarried or not, have had some type of contract. That contract could be overt, meaning that the couple talked about certain issues and arrived at some compromise each of them could live with. Or the contract could be a covert one in which there was no discussion about each spouse's opinion on certain key issues; if there are hidden differences, they come to light only when one spouse violates the contract. As in any other partnership, there are multiple issues to be explored and worked out in a marriage. For example, who should earn the money? Who should decide how it is spent, and who should take care of it? If both spouses work outside the home, is each spouse's say equal or only commensurate with his or her dollar contribution?

Related to the monetary issue are decisions and expectations about work. Does one spouse or do both spouses work? What kind of work is considered acceptable? When children are added to the family, how does their presence change employment patterns?

Children are an oft thought about but seldom mentioned issue for new couples. What are the criteria that determine whether or not one has children? Perhaps in one spouse's culture, financial readiness or the approval and blessings of both sets of in-laws are sufficient; the other spouse may come from a culture in which there is a belief that the very act of marrying out removes the possibility of children. If the spouses agreed to have children, how was that decision reached? How did they decide how many to have? One potential area for conflict in interfaith marriages is when one spouse maintains the belief that one has as many children as God intended one to have; one comes to know this simply by not interfering with nature. In other words, the spouse is against the use of birth control. Another issue involving children is discipline: Who makes the rules about the children? Who exercises the discipline, and who decides what type of discipline is appropriate?

Determining a comfortable level of intimacy is difficult in any relationship. Differences in cultural values can add a level of complexity to an already difficult task. Although marrying for romantic love is not the basis for many unions, once one is married there seems to be a fairly universal expectation of the production of progeny. Whether sex is seen as the means to a specific end (namely, children) or whether it is part of the definition of romantic love, sex does play a central role in marriage. Each spouse has definite ideas about whether or not the relationship should be monogamous, about when they should have sex and how often, about who should initiate it, and about what type of sexual activity is permissible. This area can be particularly sensitive in the case of intermarriage. As the reader will see in the section on motivational theories for cross-cultural marriage, one variable that does not bode well for a solid relationship is when one spouse is chosen solely on the basis of sexual stereotypes about male or female members of that culture harbored by the other spouse (Davidson, 1992).

Another area to explore is expectations about household responsibilities. Who does the housework? Is the work divided along traditional, stereotyped lines? Other areas include relaxation time, time spent with family, and the handling of holidays. How is free time spent? Is it spent alone or apart? If it is spent together, what is done and who decides that? How often do the clients see their respective families? Are there holidays observed by one family that are not observed by the other?

It should be noted that there is no evidence to date that indicates that intermarried couples have more trouble than other couples negotiating and finally compromising on these issues. In fact, clinical experience indicates that because of the intermarried couple's greater awareness of their differences on one level (race, culture, religion), they may be less apt to make assumptions about their spouse's opinions on other levels.

Examining the extent to which each spouse's expectations for the marriage correlate with what he or she has outlined as cultural or normative will also provide therapists with a rough estimation of level of acculturation. In addition, the extent to which each spouse's expectations correlate with the other's, and are more overt than covert, gives a therapist information about the couple's communication style. And finally, in areas where the couple has already reached a compromise, the therapist can explore the skills this couple has for conflict resolution.

LEVEL OF ACCULTURATION

It has been strongly recommended by Dana (1993) that prior to any assessment of individual clients in a cross-cultural situation, some measurement of acculturation should be done. *Acculturation* has been defined as the degree of integration of new cultural patterns into the original cultural patterns (Dana, 1993, cited in Paniagua, 1994, p. 8). Younger people tend to have higher levels of acculturation than older people. Newer immigrants have lower levels of acculturation than less recent immigrants (Berry, Kim, Minde, & Mok, 1987). In general, any family who has greater access to the new culture (through work, school, etc.) will have higher levels of acculturation (Paniagua, 1994). This information can be obtained informally or formally through the use of existing acculturation scales (Paniagua, 1994).

EXTERNAL SOURCES OF STRESS

Although not all intermarried couples in therapy are there because of problems related to their differences, an assessment should be made of possible past or present sources of stress that are a direct outgrowth of those differences. Until 1967, interracial marriages were against the law in the United States, and so harassment and incarceration by law enforcement personnel was a very real threat (Kouri & Lasswell, 1993). Even though this law is no longer considered constitutional, its banishment has done nothing to stem the tide of negative public opinion. Reactions to mixed marriages have ranged from verbal comments in public from complete strangers to acts of violence (Rosenblatt, Karis, & Powell, 1995). Some couples have been unable to find a place to live because of housing discrimination; others have suffered a loss of income due to discrimination in the workplace.

Perhaps the most frequently experienced source of stress for the intermarried couple is social isolation. In some cases, the couple is cut off from one or both families. Additionally, there may be rejection from peers. It may be difficult for the couple to decide whose friends to socialize with.

When intermarried couples have children they must make decisions about the racial, ethnic, or religious identity of those children. We live in a society that dictates that we label and pigeonhole ourselves, and often, there are no categories on the forms that we fill out to indicate a combination.

The responses to these stressors vary from couple to couple as well as from individual to individual. Some cope with these negative reactions by limiting the places they go and the people they have contact with. These individuals create a circumscribed world consisting of people whose approval they already have. This cuts down on the chance that they will encounter anyone whose views on intermarriage represent an unknown quantity (Rosenblatt et al., 1995). Others leave the safety of such a close-knit group and take the chance of being exposed to vitriolic responses. However, they cope by minimizing the importance of the people voicing these comments or by denying the impact such comments have on them (Rosenblatt et al., 1995). For some, their responses have revolved around their anger. They have confronted attacks on their marriages whenever and wherever they have occurred. This has been cathartic for many individuals, whereas for others it has planted seeds of anger of such magnitude that the individual is unable to let go of the anger and get on with his or her life (Rosenblatt et al., 1995).

Not unlike other individuals who have felt persecuted, some intermarried couples work extra diligently to counteract whatever negative stereotypes exist about them and their relationship. Other intermarried couples do not concern themselves with the negative stereotypes. Not to be confused with those couples in denial, these couples recognize the problems and make a conscious decision to use the stress as a tool to strengthen their relationship (Rosenblatt et al., 1995).

ASSESSMENT OF THE POSITIVE

An interesting and often overlooked area for all couples is what the couple considers to be the positive aspects of their relationship. There is such a bias in the helping professions on focusing on what is wrong and what is not working that we often overlook what is right with the relationship and what does work. A natural extension of such a discussion could include any advantages the couple sees to being intermarried. Ho (1990) lists the following advantages to an intermarried union:

More thorough preparation for marriage.
A greater degree of commitment.
A greater degree of self-other differentiation.
A greater degree of acceptance, tolerance, and respect.
Broader opportunities for learning and growth.
Greater opportunities for children.
Children more accepting of differences in others (pp. 19–20).

MOTIVATION FOR INTERMARRIAGE

The existing literature on intermarriage cites numerous theories that have been posited to explain the choice of an exogamous marital partner. Therapists need to be careful about adopting any of these explanations and applying them to the couple they are seeing in treatment.

One hypothesis, described extensively by Porterfield (1973, 1982), suggests that people who intermarry do so as a form of pathological rebellion. The conflict they have with their parents is so intense that they desire revenge in the worst way. They choose a marital partner who belongs to the group their parents would find most unsuitable and degrading to have as a member of the family. Other theorists suggest that it is a part of human nature to be preoccupied with the forbidden (Ray, 1976, 1980). Historically, there have always been certain combinations of people who fell into this category. A great deal has been written about the sexual and love relationships between Blacks and Whites. The fascination with these unions has been due in part to the many laws that existed to forbid them. But even before the laws there was a need to separate the races and denigrate Black people to justify their enslavement. The English term coined to describe the union of a man and woman of different races is miscegenation. According to these theorists, the long history in the United States of attempting to keep the races apart has rendered members of one race exotic, mysterious, and desirable to members of the other race. Part of the mystery is about the sexual prowess of men and women of color. Stereotypes abound also about Asian women and their knowledge of the sexual arts.

Many sociologists have examined the existing social class structure in this country and found that some racial and cultural groups are overrepresented in a particular class. Given this fact, it is conceivable that a person in the underclass marries out to achieve social and economic mobility.

Proponents of the structural approach are of the opinion that people who choose exogamous partners are really no different from people who choose endogamous partners. The implication is that people intermarry because over the years the opportunities for people of different races and cultures to interact have increased. Because of this increase in contact, people have had a chance to get to know people they assumed were different on a first-hand basis, and discovered similarities in values and interests (Farber, 1973; Kouri & Lasswell, 1993).

McGoldrick and Garcia Preto (1984) provide us with a family systems perspective on why people intermarry: "They are seeking a rebalance in the characteristics of their own background.... Those who marry out may also be seeking to solve a family dilemma. They may be attempting to detriangle from an intense emotional relationship in the family of origin" (pp. 350–351).

What is clear is that no single theory can explain the motivation of the variety of people who intermarry. Many of the theories fail to take into account individual differences. Furthermore, some of these theories are unsubstantiated in any empirical way. Finally, theories that may have been applicable at one time may have lost their applicability over time.

BICULTURAL EXISTENCE

This area of assessment refers to how the couple handles living in two worlds. An important aspect of each person's development is his or her ethnic identity, racial identity (Helms, 1985), and/or religious identity. In intimate relationships, there is sometimes a romantic desire on the part of spouses to cast aside individuality and forge a new whole.

Problems can develop when important aspects of the individual are sacrificed for the sake of the couple. Family therapists use the term *enmeshment* to describe relationships in which individual autonomy is missing. In family and couples therapy sessions, this enmeshment can be seen when the therapist directs a question to one family member and that person responds in the first person plural: "We think" or "We feel." This individual speaks as though the family is one. Enmeshment can occur in endogamous couples as well; however, the difference with exogamous couples lies in the fact that part of the assessment process includes attention to racial, ethnic, and religious aspects of each spouse's identity.

The therapist will be interested in whether or not one spouse's racial identity is more dominant than the other's. If the racial identity of one spouse is more powerful, does that power imbalance mirror the relationship between those races in the larger society? For example, in Black-White interracial marriages, the children are usually considered Black and the families tend to live and socialize in Black communities. From the child's perspective, at least, the Black identity seems to play the dominant role. It is important and helpful for the therapist to understand how it was decided which identity would dominate and whether or not things changed with the birth of children.

In assessing the coping skills of a couple one cannot overlook how racial, ethnic, or religious differences emerge in conflict. Are derogatory racial remarks or religious stereotypes used in arguments? Are negative family traits attributed more often to one group than the other? Are racial slurs slipped in a conversation passive-aggressively through the use of humor (Rosenblatt et al., 1995)?

When one spouse is a member of an ethnic, racial, or religious minority and the other spouse is not, how similar are their views about racism (Rosenblatt et al., 1995)? Differences on this subject can be very emotionally charged when two people are strangers. The meaning of the same subject can increase exponentially when the two people discussing it are intimates.

FORMAL ASSESSMENT INSTRUMENTS

Standardized formal assessment instruments are frequently utilized by therapists doing couples work. Many of these instruments are useful in terms of targeting the problems. They have also been used pre- and posttherapy as a way to measure change. And when both spouses fill out the same instrument, the therapist has been able to gauge the degree of agreement between them on certain issues. Regardless of how these assessment devices are used, it is important to examine the appropriateness of their use with certain populations.

If a therapist chooses to use a scale in work with people from other cultures, it is necessary to know whether the scale was normed on that group or whether a sufficient number of the target group was represented in the standardization sample (Armour-Thomas, 1992; Suzuki & Kugler, 1995). Does the scale have content validity for the people under consideration? In other words, given the fact that race, ethnicity, culture, gender, and religion can influence what one sees as a problem, therapists should be sure that the scale has not overlooked areas that may be important to their clients.

Other issues highlighted by Suzuki and Kugler (1995) concern the existence of conceptual equivalence and the existence of versions of the scale in other languages. If there is no formally translated version of the scale, one has to be careful about the use of translators. A frequent problem is the lack of verbatim translation. Some translators may summarize or inject their own meaning into a statement. This has a definite impact on the responses one obtains.

SPECIAL ISSUES

REMARRIED FAMILIES

The absence of a blueprint for how remarried families are supposed to act toward one another can create a great deal of confusion. One major problem is the fact that remarried families are predicated on one of two life cycle events (death of a spouse or divorce) that result in loss. When the remaining spouse, in the case of death, or the divorced spouses choose new partners, the number of people in the family and the number of existing households increase. Myriad boundary issues can develop as family members worry about whether there is sufficient love to go around and whether they are really considered members of the family. These issues exist when the families are racially, ethnically, or religiously homogeneous. If one of the spouses in a homogeneous marriage decides to marry out the second time, there can be additional identity issues for the children, particularly if they do not resemble the stepparent.

Case Example

Mr. and Mrs. Green are an African American couple. Mr. Green was married before to another African American woman and they had two girls. The second Mrs. Green was married before to a Caucasian man of Swiss descent. They had two boys. Physically, the two boys resembled their father: blond hair, light eyes, and European features. At the point of remarriage, the new household consisted of two African American adults who were brown-skinned and the two boys who were so light-skinned as to appear White. The girls from Mr. Green's previous marriage were older and lived on their own. When the two boys went to school they were often teased by classmates who suggested that they were adopted because they did not resemble either their biological mother or stepfather.

FIDELITY

One danger in intermarried couples is the chance that infidelity on the part of either spouse may be attributed to cultural stereotypes. Another danger lies in differing expectations about the issue of monogamy. It is important for therapists to explore how infidelity is viewed in each spouse's culture. Is the infidelity of women viewed differently from the same behavior in men? What are the consequences of infidelity? Is there any culturally sanctioned way to make amends for the affair and rebuild the relationship?

In addition to this type of discussion, the therapist must be careful about being more concerned about the affair than the spouses. In some cultures, extramarital relationships are overtly condemned but covertly condoned. Sometimes, affairs are utilized with discretion to deal with the dichotomous roles assigned to a woman in a given society; for example, there may be a belief that men should marry women who are pure and virginal. In such a marriage, sex is for the purpose of procreation. Any sexual act that does not or cannot result in the production of children may be viewed as lewd. Therefore, men who feel that they must satisfy these sexual appetites do so with other women.

Certainly every intermarried couple warrants their own thorough assessment. Such an assessment would ideally be free of the following common myths and stereotypes:

1. All intermarried couples are alike.
2. All intermarried couples choose their partners for the same reasons.
3. All the "reasons" for intermarriage stem from some type of pathology.
4. The racial, cultural, or religious differences between the partners constitutes their major problem or reason for seeking treatment.
5. Intermarried couples are by definition at risk for more problems and pathology than non-intermarried couples.

PART THREE

CROSS-CULTURAL ISSUES IN TREATMENT

CHAPTER 5

The Treatment of Culturally Diverse Clients

THERAPIST'S SELF-EXAMINATION

BEFORE WORKING with culturally diverse clients it is important for therapists to examine their motives for doing this work. A differentiation should be made between self-serving agendas and altruistic sentiments. Clients who are members of minority cultures can end up satisfying a therapist's need for power and self-aggrandizement that is not being met elsewhere. This can manifest itself in a misuse of power: differentially enforcing the rules concerning the parameters of treatment (length of session, scheduling of session, etc.); elevating one's position as therapist while belittling the patient; insisting on being addressed by a title (Dr., Mr., Mrs., etc.) but addressing clients by their first names; and so on. Does the therapist work with people from the poorer classes or minorities who are victims of racism and oppression to feel good about himself or herself (Boyd-Franklin, 1989; Pinderhughes, 1989)? Pinderhughes (1989) offers the following suggestions to begin to remedy these problems:

1. Therapists who have dislike for or lack respect for certain groups of people should not work with them.
2. Therapists should be willing to make themselves vulnerable, whether that means letting the client know that they don't know everything or being less directive from time to time.

3. Therapists need to carefully examine the many dimensions of who they are: racially, ethnically, culturally, in regard to gender, socioeconomic level, access to education, and so on. For most people, power is not uniform: one can be powerful in one area of their lives and powerless in others. For example, a Jewish man may be cognizant of his powerlessness as a target of racial discrimination but be unaware of his power as a White person in a country where the majority are White. A female therapist may be in touch with her powerlessness along gender lines but unaware of her power along racial lines.

4. Therapists need to believe that they have as much to learn from their clients as their clients have to learn from them. Therapists cannot enter the therapeutic relationship on an ethnocentric and paternalistic mission. By that, we mean that therapists cannot approach therapy with the idea that the values of their culture are the best and only way to do things and that therefore the clients must be made to change.

5. Therapists can help some clients from minority groups not to idealize the mainstream culture.

6. Therapists can help clients to appreciate their own cultures and not "buy into" or support negative cultural images.

ISSUES IN THE EARLY STAGES OF THERAPY OR BEGINNING THERAPY

There are myriad issues to be considered during the initial session with a family or individual who is culturally dissimilar from the therapist. One of those issues concerns the choice of labels. How does the client want the therapist to refer to the ethnic group to which the client belongs? We have encouraged supervisees to ask their clients. It avoids the risk of offending the client early in the relationship, and many clients view the inquiry as a sign of respect.

Another issue has to do with how important racial or ethnic similarity between therapist and client is to the client. The empirical research on this topic has been primarily in two areas: How important is the therapist's race or ethnicity to the client? and If the therapist's race is an important factor, do clients have a preference (Davis & Proctor,

1989)? In one study, when clients were given a number of therapist characteristics and then asked to rank order them in terms of importance, race was ranked fifth (Davis & Proctor, 1989). In their review of the literature, Davis and Proctor (1989) found that when other therapist characteristics such as level of education, personality, individual style, age, perceived attitudinal similarity, and years of clinical experience were controlled for, clients did not seem to show a preference for a therapist of the same race.

In sum, these studies and others have been inconclusive. Many of the studies did not use actual clients in the research. Often, the researchers failed to control for the length of time the individual had been in therapy with that therapist. And sometimes, studies that were being compared had not asked the same questions of their participants (Davis & Proctor, 1989). Despite the need for more controlled studies, there does seem to be agreement that in cases of cross racial therapeutic dyads, the subject of racial differences must be addressed (Boyd-Franklin, 1989).

The failure of White therapists working with clients of color to bring up the issue of race has been explained in several ways. In some cases, White therapists do not recognize race as an important issue; Whites in the United States do not include skin color as part of their self-definition. For some people of color, just the opposite is true. In other instances, White therapists report that they deliberately do not talk about racial differences because they want their clients of color to feel that they (therapists) are color-blind (Davis & Proctor, 1989). Finally, there are White therapists who are extremely fearful of the reactions of clients of color. Part of their anxiety is due to their anticipation of angry responses and client rejection. These therapists are often at a loss as to how to handle such a discussion even in the absence of anger and conflict.

It seems advisable for the topic of racial differences to be brought up by the therapist early in treatment. Waiting too long may result in mistrust and anxiety and contribute to dropout.

It should be noted that the discussion of race is not limited to cross-racial therapeutic dyads. Therapists who are the same race as their clients should also have this discussion. It is important for the therapist to come away with an understanding of what it means to the client that they are racially similar. What assumptions might clients make about common ground shared between them (B. Greene, personal communication, 1992)?

Another issue to address at the beginning of treatment is what meaning the individual attaches to the word *therapist.* This discussion provides the therapist with information about the client's expectations. If the individual is not self-referred, does he or she understand the referral process, the consequences of going to therapy (what it means to receive a diagnosis, who can have access to records, etc.), and the consequences of not going to therapy?

One way to enhance one's understanding and appreciation of a client's culture is by gaining knowledge about family structure: How is *family* defined, or what is meant by family to people from this culture? Is the family organized hierarchically or vertically? What is the actual and perceived distribution of power? What do the roles of men, women, and children entail? How are the elderly perceived and treated? What are the fears and concerns regarding young people? The answers to some of these questions can be helpful in determining who are the key people to include in a family session. It is also helpful in terms of deciphering or assigning meaning to seating arrangements in the office. It can also prevent a therapist from pathologizing certain communication patterns. One's position in the family can determine whom one is allowed to speak to, when, and in what manner. Therapists may inadvertently offend by addressing initially the wrong family member or by speaking too long to a "less significant" family member.

Whether the client is a recent immigrant or has been in this country for many years, it is important to determine his or her level of acculturation. If a formal assessment tool is desired, Burman, Hough, Karno, Escobar, and Telles (1987) have developed the Brief Acculturation Scale, which has been found to be most helpful for a general population; of course, there are other scales that have been developed for use with specific populations, such as Latinos.

When working with clients who are members of groups that have experienced some form of oppression, it is a good idea when terminating the first session to utilize a model of strength. All too often, therapists have modeled themselves after members of the medical community and worked from a deficit model: looking for what is wrong, what needs to be fixed. Clients from oppressed groups are all too familiar with what people think is "wrong" with them. Positive feedback stressing the individual's strengths will be much more productive.

USE OF TRANSLATORS

A substantial barrier to the provision of services to culturally diverse people is the lack of frontline staff (receptionists and secretaries) who can speak different languages. It is often intimidating to make that initial call to a clinic or therapist's office requesting services; clients can be further intimidated when they cannot make themselves understood by the person on the other end of the phone. Clients for whom English is not a first language are at a distinct disadvantage. They are unable to make the usual initial inquiries made by prospective clients—questions about the staff, the fee structure, and the availability of appointments.

If the client manages to overcome those initial problems, the next barrier to treatment has to do with who, among the professional staff, is in a position to conduct an assessment interview and/or subsequent therapy sessions. Clinics and agencies are tremendously understaffed. The staff that does exist is usually lacking in bilingual therapists. When there is no one on the clinical staff who speaks the same language as the client, therapists have to compromise. One way they have done this has been to utilize nonclinical staff in the agency as translators. These nonclinical staff members include secretaries, receptionists, and housekeeping personnel. But when the language problem has been overcome, other problems may present themselves. First, a client may not be forthcoming about reasons for seeking treatment in the presence of a nonprofessional. Second, one should not expect that the nonprofessional staff member is cognizant of the rules of confidentiality that govern the psychotherapeutic relationship. And finally, there is the issue of the quality of the translation. Translators may be unfamiliar with the words or phrases that would precisely translate the professional terminology being used. Communication may be further complicated if the translator paraphrases what the client says. The therapist would have no way of knowing this and could end up operating from inaccurate information.

Another scenario that the therapist may have to deal with is the client's bringing a family member and/or friend to serve as translator. The obvious advantage is the individual's fluency with the language. The disadvantages include the violation of the client's right to privacy and the possibility of omissions or additions in the translation that are guided by the family member's feeling about the client and his or her situation. For example, a woman who is coming to talk about the unhappiness she experiences in her marriage is not going to want to have her husband translate; an adolescent having problems with his or her parents is not going to welcome the parents acting in the capacity of translator.

Obviously, the ideal situation is to have a therapist who is similar to the client in cultural background. This therapist would speak not only the same language but the same dialect. However, since the probability of such therapist-client matches is very low, most of the time translators will have to be used. Whenever possible, translators should be professionals rather than family, friends, or office staff. Translations should be verbatim, and "edited summations" of the client's words should be avoided. In much the same way that English interviews are conducted, therapeutic jargon and words should be kept to a minimum. In instances where the use of psychological terms is unavoidable, the therapist can try to discuss problems in translation before the session with the client (Westermeyer, 1993).

Therapists who consider themselves conversant in a second language must be mindful of the degree of familiarity they have with colloquialisms. There are phrases in every language that are not directly translatable.

THE CHOICE OF THERAPEUTIC MODALITY

There is no conclusive research to date to suggest that one therapeutic modality is better than another for treating individuals from diverse cultural backgrounds. Until that research is done, therapists will have to combine their clinical skills with their knowledge of the client's culture to determine the advantages and disadvantages of one modality over another.

FAMILY THERAPY

Family therapy is a particularly good modality for people who are members of cultures where family needs and goals take precedence over individual needs and goals. The Asian family is a good example of this: "The emphasis on community and family as the organizing social structure exerts fundamental pressure on the individual to subordinate rather than elevate personal need. The sense of belonging and obligation to the family extends throughout the family network, as well as forward to posterity and backward to ancestors" (Shon & Ja, 1982, cited in McGoldrick, Pearce, & Giordano, 1982, pp. 208–228).

The specific school of Bowenian family therapy (see Chapter 6) has the potential to be very efficacious with clients in which intergenerational legacies and the power of the past are important (Boyd-Franklin & Garcia-Preto, 1994). Families who prefer more present-oriented and crisis-focused work are apt to be more amenable to Minuchen's structural family therapy. This orientation can be particularly useful with many immigrant families, as it addresses some of the boundary issues and cross-generational alliances that may become blurred and confused through the course of immigration. It examines family members' roles to make sure they are clearly articulated and understood. Often, family members put in a new place believe that they have new responsibilities.

Family treatment may be contraindicated for individuals from cultures where separation and individuation are highly prized. These individuals may not want to be seen within the context of their families. Axelson (1993) states that "Anglo-Saxon Americans, beginning with the English, established the base that was to become mainstream culture in the United States. Some features of traditional Protestant values [include] individual direction, determination, independence and autonomy" (p. 92). Another possible contraindication for family therapy has more to do with the therapist than the clients and their culture. A therapist's lack of familiarity with different family structures might lead to pathologizing some families' ways of functioning.

GROUP THERAPY

Group treatment is another modality to consider. Davis and Proctor (1989) state that "it does appear that a significant number of those [group] models advocated for use with minorities are those that focus on cultural sensitivity, concreteness, active leadership, immediate attention to problem resolution, and a clear recognition of the importance of the environment as a contributing factor to the client's problems" (p. 115). Therapists will want to keep in mind the composition of the group. If the group is heterogeneous, are there more than one or two members of an ethnic minority group present? This is important because these two members may get scapegoated in the process. The purpose of the group also determines composition. Groups that are topic-specific for a particular ethnic group are likely to be more successful when there is group homogeneity. For example, a group of African American women focused on relationship and self-esteem issues is going to proceed differently if Anglo women join the group.

Language is something else to keep in mind. Clients may be members of a broad ethnic category (e.g., Asians) that has much diversity (Japanese, Chinese, Koreans, Vietnamese, Laotians, etc.). To simply lump these diverse people in a group ignores the language barrier.

INDIVIDUAL THERAPY

The individual treatment modality has its advantages and disadvantages. A distinct disadvantage to seeing some clients alone is when they come from cultures (such as most non-Westernized societies) in which individuality and autonomy are either discouraged or at the very least not of primary importance. One advantage, however, is the opportunity such a modality affords an individual who is ambivalent about the amount of closeness he or she wants to maintain with the family. For example, there are issues that arise when successive generations become more acculturated than their elders. Sometimes children, adolescents, and young adults attempt to work out their disagreements with the older generation by seeking more autonomy.

The stigma attached to mental illness and the seeking of psychological services is still very much in effect. This fear can be amplified when a client is from a culture that looks unfavorably on the idea of therapy. In these instances, individual treatment allows the client to get the help he or she needs without having to deal with family censure.

CHOICE OF THEORETICAL ORIENTATION

Therapists who do cross-cultural work often wonder which theoretical orientation is most effective with which cultural groups. There has been insufficient research to adequately answer that question. What does seem evident from clinical practice is that it is not an all or none proposition: each theoretical orientation has something that adds to or detracts from its usefulness with a given population.

COGNITIVE THERAPY

Cognitive behavior therapy has a number of things to offer a therapist working with clients who have been oppressed and discriminated against and who feel powerless in the larger society. The therapeutic relationship is defined in such a way that the therapist is not presented as an all-powerful and all-knowing figure. The status of clients is elevated. "Clients reinforce themselves, setbacks are seen as an opportunity for learning, and there is no adherence to a medical model looking for illness and weakness" (Lewis, 1994, pp. 229–230). Lewis (1994) points out, however, that the major disadvantage to cognitive behavior therapy and theory is the absence of a discussion of race, gender, and ethnicity.

FEMINIST THERAPY

At the other end of the continuum is feminist therapy. Feminists call for reconstruction of terms and development of models that can better illuminate the contradictions and consequences at the point of interaction of gender, family, and society (Wright, 1992). To their credit, one of the major points that feminist family therapists have made is the fact that the notion of family generally referred to in psychology excludes and labels as deviant a vast number of cultures. Also to their credit has been the focus on sociocultural factors in therapy (Espin, 1994) and the attempt made to empower clients. Despite all this, however, therapists need to be alert to the myths many cultures and/or individuals within those cultures have about what it means to be a feminist, such as the following: feminists only see women in therapy; feminists are only interested in male bashing; feminist therapists use therapy to devalue the roles of mothers and homemakers; and feminist therapists are trying to convince women in therapy that they do not need men in their lives.

PSYCHOANALYSIS

Psychoanalytic and psychodynamic therapies frequently have been accused of being elitist, placing therapy out of reach for certain cultural groups and socioeconomic classes. Rather than debate that issue here, we would prefer to focus on one of the very important contributions psychoanalytic theory has made to working with people of color, namely, the delineation of racially related defense mechanisms. Ridley (1995) offers the following list:

1. *Color blindness*—an illusion that the minority client is no different from nonminority clients.
2. *Color consciousness*—the premise that the problems of members of ethnic minorities all stem from their minority status.
3. *Cultural transference*—when the client transfers feelings and attitudes developed from interactions with people of another race onto the therapist.
4. *Cultural countertransference*—when the therapist transfers onto the client feelings and attitudes developed about people of the client's race.
5. *Cultural ambivalence*—the therapist's desire to help minorities but with a need to control and manipulate and be in a generally superior position.
6. *Overidentification*—when minority therapists overidentify with minority clients' experiences with racism and narrowly define the problem as racially based.
7. *Identification with the oppressor*—when minority therapists deny their minority status because it is too painful and identify themselves with White people (pp. 67–68, copyright © 1995, reprinted by permission of Sage Publications, Inc.).

The factors listed above take into consideration those things that majority and minority therapists bring into the therapy room.

FAMILY THERAPY

Family therapy has some distinct advantages. It maintains a systemic viewpoint that doesn't look for illness or to stigmatize an individual. This is particularly important in cultures where the notion of going to a therapist is a negative one. The focus on family takes the therapist in the direction of getting information about family structure, roles, and distribution of power. However, one should keep in mind the fact that family therapists are not immune from making assumptions and judgments about optimal family structure, optimal family functioning, and development.

CULTURE-BOUND SYNDROMES

Culture-bound syndromes are clusters of symptoms that have been labeled and defined by a specific culture's belief system regarding illness. The list below was compiled by Paniagua (1994) from the work of Griffin and Baker (1993), Rubel, O'Nell, and Collado-Ardon (1984), and Simons and Hughes (1993).

1. *Ataque de nervios* (Hispanic)—an out-of-consciousness state resulting from evil spirits.
2. *Falling-out* (African American)—seizurelike symptoms resulting from traumatic events.
3. *Ghost sickness* (American Indian)—weakness, dizziness resulting from the action of witches and evil forces.
4. *Hwa-byung* (Asian)—pain in the upper abdomen, fear of death, tiredness resulting from the imbalance between reality and anger.
5. *Koro* (Asian)—a man's desire to grasp his penis, resulting from fear that it will retract into his body and cause death.
6. *Taijinkyofusho* (Asian)—guilt about embarrassing others; timidity resulting from the feeling that one's appearance, odor, facial expressions are offensive to other people.
7. *Malpuesto* (African American and Hispanic)—hex, rootwork, or voodoo death resulting from the power of people who use evil spirits.
8. *Susto, espanto, pasmo, miedo* (Hispanic)—tiredness and weakness resulting from frightening and startling experiences.
9. *Wacinko* (American Indian)—anger, withdrawal, mutism, suicide resulting from reaction to disappointment and interpersonal problems.
10. *Wind/cold illness* (Hispanic and Asian)—a fear of the cold and the wind; feeling weakness and susceptibility to illness resulting from the belief that natural and supernatural elements are not balanced (p. 113, copyright © 1994, reprinted by permission of Sage Publications, Inc.).

Just because a client exhibits culture-related syndromes does not mean that he or she does not need psychological or psychiatric care. On the other hand, there are times when a culture-related syndrome could be indicative of a psychiatric disorder, as in the following example.

RELIGIOUS BELIEF AND ITS IMPACT ON PERSONALITY ASSESSMENT

In attempting to understand the causes of mental illness, many immigrants, especially those from Eastern cultures and immigrant islands, rarely invoke psychological explanations. On the contrary, mental illness is attributed to some form of spiritual restlessness meted out to the individual via a vengeful spirit. Many cultures have a belief in some form of witchcraft that can be worked on someone by an enemy to cause various forms of harm, usually out of envy or to take revenge. Folk belief says that when a person is "possessed," a spirit enters the individual's body, such that the behavior of the person becomes the behavior of the spirit. It is felt that the more suggestible a person is, the more likely he or she is to become "possessed."

Philippe and Romain (1979) found females are more likely than males to become "possessed." These folk beliefs are deeply embedded in the culture and can exert a profound influence on people's lives. Many individuals wear a guard, receive spiritual baths (herbal baths with holy water), and have a priest or minister bless the home or throw salt around the house to protect themselves from these evil forces. These beliefs are accepted by most sectors of society, transcending race, class, age, and gender. Over the past 10 years, we have seen several clients go to a spiritist while simultaneously seeking psychological help. For example, a woman had sought therapy because her sons had suddenly begun to misbehave "as soon as my mother-in-law had moved into the house." Since her mother-in-law had never accepted her, she attributed the children's misbehavior to her mother-in-law's "evil eye." She talked openly about her suspicions, assuming that the therapist not only understood but would be able to help her in exorcising the children. When the role of a psychologist was explained to her, she was very disappointed that the therapist would not even be able to accompany her to the spiritist. She felt that the problem with her sons was not a psychological one, but a spiritual one. Given the intensity of her belief, we recommended that she seek the counsel of a spiritist first and then resume therapy afterwards if the negative behaviors of her sons continued after the "bad spirits" were removed from them. She was receptive to this idea and more trusting of the psychological treatment process after she had taken the children to the spiritual healer.

Thus, a therapist who hears a parent say "my child is not conforming because an evil spirit is on him" and then sees the child wearing a chain with a big cross (guard), should not be alarmed. Similarly, when a woman attributes her husband's infidelity or lack of familial interest to that fact that "someone gave him something to eat that has him *tottlebey* [stupid]," she is expressing a cultural assessment of her husband's behavior.

The individual who says "I see the evil spirit in my house" or "the evil spirit talked to me" is not necessarily hallucinating, nor is the individual who says "God came to me and told me to give up my job, so I did" necessarily delusional. If mental health professionals are not aware of the folk system, they may misdiagnose a client or devalue or demean folk culturological behaviors. The major point for therapists in assessing psychiatric problems in immigrant families is to try to determine the difference between "being possessed" and true mental illness. When dealing with immigrants, the area of most confusion is in the accurate assessment of schizophrenia, particularly paranoid schizophrenia.

Differential Diagnosis: Spirit Possession or Schizophrenia?

To make a differential diagnosis, it is first necessary to do a thorough historical assessment of the individual's psychosocial, behavioral, and cognitive functioning. Schizophrenics often exhibit dysfunctions in thought, form, perceptions, affect, sense of self, interpersonal functioning, and psychomotor behavior. To be given a diagnosis of schizophrenia, at least two of the following elements must have existed for at least six months: delusions, hallucinations, incoherence or marked loosening of associations, catatonic behavior, or flat or grossly inappropriate affect. In addition, functioning in such areas as work, self-care, and social relations must be markedly low. Lefley (1979) found that the responses of "possessed" victims reflected little of the impulsiveness, lability, and free-flowing emotionality that characterize schizophrenia. In fact, while "their consciousness is altered, it is not dissociated in the form of a split personality," as is commonly seen with schizophrenics (p. 120). Schizophrenia is generally treated with antipsychotic drugs, which are useful for eliminating the delusions and hallucinations and alleviating thought disorder.

While acculturating, many immigrants may exhibit psychotic symptoms due to situational stress. Regarding folk beliefs, it is enough to say that it is a pattern of social behavior that has been learned (by constant exposure from childhood onwards) and in which people have been conditioned to believe. In other words, it is culturally sanctioned and even considered to be a spiritually uplifting experience. "Possession is not abnormal, it is normal" (Wittkower, 1964, p. 76). For people who endorse the spiritual unrest view, the duration can range from one day to several years. The major point is that many people from culturally diverse backgrounds believe a spiritist can remove the evil spirit and free the individual from this "evil force." Therefore, whereas schizophrenics have difficulty eradicating the psychosis, the "possessed" ought not.

THE INDIVIDUAL VERSUS THE GROUP

Who are we really treating when a client walks through the door? Do we see, for example, an Asian, or do we see a person who happens to be of Asian extraction? The difference is not simply one of semantics. In the former situation (seeing the Asian), we run the risk of treating the client as though he or she is a member of a homogeneous group (in this case, the group called Asians). Within-group differences such as country of origin, ethnic identification, socioeconomic status, and others may be ignored. In fact, a problem with some of the research that is conducted using culturally diverse samples is that generalizations get made about a particular culture when in fact some intervening variable (such as SES) is really responsible for between-group differences. To a certain extent, when we get a new client we must (as the statisticians would say) conduct a multivariate analysis. Comas-Diaz and Greene (1994) made this very point in their book when they examined the intersection of gender and ethnicity. The lesson to be learned is that people do not behave in one particular way, but a multiplicity of ways that make them rich and complicated.

CHAPTER 6

Multicultural/Multimodal/
Multisystems (Multi-CMS)
Approach in Treating Culturally
Diverse Families

CURRENT MAJOR APPROACHES IN COUNSELING
CULTURALLY DIFFERENT FAMILIES

ECOGNIZING THAT it is impossible for any therapist to understand the traditions, values, and languages of all immigrant groups, Gopaul-McNicol (1993, 1997a, 1997b) offers a conceptual, operational guide that can be implemented across diverse groups. This chapter explores several treatment techniques that can apply to immigrants, with particular attention to the model developed by Gopaul-McNicol (1993), the Multicultural/Multimodal/Multisystems (Multi-CMS) approach.

MULTICULTURAL COUNSELING

Multicultural counseling has become a popular concept among practitioners and researchers because it is a way to acknowledge cultural diversity between therapist and client. Dillard (1983) includes in the definition of *culture* a shared belief system, behavioral styles, symbols, and attitudes within a social group. Assimilating to a particular culture is a slow process that involves the stage of acculturation, that is, adopting some dominant social and cultural norms and possibly losing a sense of cultural identity with one's original culture. In attempting to conduct multicultural counseling, the goal must be to assist the culturally different client to adapt to or reshape his or her psychosocial environment (Dillard, 1983). Sue (1981) examined the underlying principles in attempting to counsel the culturally different. His major point was the importance of the therapist's being knowledgeable about the client's culture and lifestyle to provide culturally responsive forms of treatment. Sue and Zane (1987) emphasized that changes had to do with the process of "match or fit." Treatment should match or fit the cultural lifestyles or experiences of clients to prevent premature termination and underutilization of services and ultimately to result in positive outcomes. Thus, knowledge of the culture, the formulation of culturally relevant, consistent strategies, credibility (the client's perception of the therapist as an effective and trustworthy helper), and giving (the client's perception that something was received from the therapeutic encounter) are all important and necessary in providing more adequate service to the culturally different.

Implicit in cross-cultural psychology is the notion of biculturalism. Many theorists view biculturalism as the healthiest identity resolution in the United States, although some view it as an abandonment of one's cultural heritage. Pedersen (1985) sees biculturalism as an addition to one's original heritage and examines the process by which cultural identity develops, since intercultural interactions influence one's behavior. Helms (1985) outlines the three stages of cultural identity.

Stage 1, the preencounter stage, is the phase before the individual's cultural awakening. In this stage, the individual is so enmeshed in the Eurocentric view that he or she idealizes White culture and degrades his or her own culture of origin. The affective state associated with stage 1 is both poor individual and poor group self-esteem.

Stage 2, the transitional phase, occurs when the individual comes to realize his or her lack of absolute acceptance by the White world. The individual goes through a period of withdrawal and cultural reassessment, ultimately deciding to become a member of his or her own cultural group. Dillard (1983) points out that in this stage, the individual sees his or her cultural systems as superior to other cultural systems. It is a stage of ethnocentrism. The affective state is one of euphoria, a sort of spiritual rebirth, as the individual tries to identify with his or her culture of origin. However, there is also confusion and sadness as the individual realizes that there has been some loss of cultural identity since he or she cannot identify with all the values of the original culture.

Stage 3, the final, or transcendent, stage occurs when the person becomes bicultural and uses the experiences from both cultural groups to best fit his or her own circumstances. In this stage, the individual is more accepting of the flaws in both cultures and does not idealize either group. Affect is less tempered, and an identity resolution is experienced. Interpersonal relations are not limited by race, culture, gender, and so forth; a broader perspective is endorsed. Self-esteem is improved. This stage is attained after one experiences an identity transformation via personal readiness and educational and cultural socialization experiences requiring cultural flexibility. Recommendations for the therapists on how to best treat individuals in these various stages are discussed later in this chapter.

MULTIMODAL THERAPY

The aim of multimodal therapy is to reduce psychological discomfort and promote individual growth by recognizing that few, if any, problems have a single cause or a single cure. Lazarus (1976) dissected human personality by examining the interaction among multiple modalities—behavior, affect, sensations, images, cognitions, interpersonal, and biological elements (BASIC IB). To make the acronym more compelling, the biological modality was redesignated D for "drugs"—BASIC ID—although it actually includes the range of medical interventions (e.g., nutrition, hygiene, exercise, medication). The multimodal assessment focuses on the behaviors that are getting in the way of the client's happiness and how one behaves when one feels (affect) a certain way, as well as what the sensations (e.g., aches and pains) are and what bearings these sensations have on behavior and feelings. In addition, the goal is to examine how one perceives one's body and self-image, how one's cognitions affect one's emotions, and what one's intellectual interests are. Who the most important people in one's life (interpersonal) are and what they are doing to one are also explored. Moreover, the focus is on any concerns one has about the state of one's health and the drugs or medication that one uses.

Educational Approach

Bowen's (1978) systems therapy, in which the therapist is portrayed as a teacher who utilizes an educational approach to therapy, is quite compatible with the perspective of many culturally diverse people's manner of securing and accepting help. This approach recognizes the value of education and research toward self-change.

Besides, Bowen's concept of the "coach" is very applicable in working with immigrant families. Rather than meeting with the family, Bowen has the person who came to therapy coach other family members into emotionally mature relationships with one another. This coaching approach has been found to be very helpful (Gopaul-McNicol, 1993), because it is difficult to get an entire family to come into therapy. Because men typically are more resistant, using a coach may be the next most effective approach. Family therapy can be quite threatening to immigrant families, who may surmise that the entire family is being seen as dysfunctional. Bowen's coaching, which makes it unnecessary for the entire family to be present simultaneously, is also useful because immigrant parents often have difficulty engaging in discussions in the presence of their children, which is the typical mode of family therapy. By using this technique, members who otherwise may not have become involved in therapy may be treated. With many culturally diverse families, Gopaul-McNicol (1993) has found that the best coach is the eldest male child. Although the mother is traditionally the intermediary between the father and the children, in the final analysis, she is expected to side with the father, especially in the presence of the children. The eldest son, by virtue of being a male and an elder offspring, is the one who can gain the respect of the younger siblings (because he himself is still in cultural transition), as well as get the attention of his parents, especially his father, because of his seniority in the hierarchical family structure.

Structural Approach

The structural approach to family therapy is mainly associated with Minuchin (1974). The focus is on boundaries, the patterns of the family, and the relationship between the family system and its wider ecological environment. An individual's symptoms are perceived as due to a family's failure to accommodate its structure to the individual's changing developmental and environmental requirements. These dysfunctional reactions to stress create problems that manifest themselves in family interrelations. The responsibility for change rests primarily on the therapist, who utilizes three strategies: challenging the symptom, challenging the family structure, and challenging the family reality. The therapist has to negotiate the family boundary in such a manner as to be given the power to be therapeutic. These boundary issues incorporate the concepts of enmeshment (some or all of the family members are relatively undifferentiated or permeable) and disengagement (family members behave in a nonchalant manner, since they have little to do with one another, because family boundaries are very rigid and impermeable).

While most families fall within the normal range, Boyd-Franklin (1989) stated that the cultural norm among Black families tends to fall within the enmeshed range. Aponte (1976), one of Minuchin's colleagues, discusses the issue of the power of some family members, who may or may not be in therapy with the identified patient. Aponte emphasizes that even if one conducts several therapy sessions with the identified patient and other family members, change may be sabotaged because of a powerful family member who did not become involved in the therapeutic process. These powerful members may influence the other members to terminate or continue treatment. Thus, the therapist is advised to explore as early as possible who the truly powerful family members are. Therapists need to find out such information as who the client goes to before making a decision, which family member has the final say on most matters (in most societies around the world, it tends to be the father), whom the client listens to most in the family, and who tends to disagree most with the client's decision. These questions can help in identifying the powerful figure who needs to be more directly involved in therapy.

MULTISYSTEMS APPROACH

Boyd-Franklin (1989) emphasized that effective therapy with African American families requires from the therapist a flexibility that allows him or her to draw from different systems theories and incorporate them into an overall treatment plan. It also requires the therapist to intervene at a variety of systems levels, such as individual, family, extended family, church, community, and social services. Boyd-Franklin's multisystems approach has been quite challenging to traditional theories in the field of mental health. Many clinicians feel that working with social service agencies and churches is the task of a social worker and not a clinician. Many therapists feel overwhelmed by the complexity of this multisystem model.

However, in working with Black families, establishing rapport and building credibility are necessary and may involve intervening in numerous systems and at many levels. This model was built on the structural family systems model of Minuchin, Montalvo, Guerney, Rosman, and Schmer (1967) and Minuchin (1974), Aponte's (1976) ecostructural approach, Aponte and Van Deusen, (1981), and the ecological approach of a number of theorists, such as Auerswald (1968), Bronfenbrenner (1977), Falicov (1988), Hartman (1978), Hartman and Laird (1983), and Holman (1983).

The multisystems approach, which comprises two main axes, is based on a concept of circularity rather than linearity, as are most treatment approaches. Axis I, the treatment process, is composed of the basic components of the therapeutic process: joining, engaging, assessing, problem solving, and interventions designed to restructure and change family systems. Each component can recur throughout the treatment process at all systems levels. Axis II, the multisystems levels, is made up of levels at which the therapist can provide treatment, such as individual, family, extended family, nonblood kin and friends, place of worship, community, social service agencies, and other outside systems.

THE INTEGRATION OF THE THREE APPROACHES

In general, treatment with immigrant families can be best understood via a comprehensive model, the Multi-CMS approach proposed by Gopaul-McNicol (1993). This approach also recognizes that within the community, the idea that "it takes a whole community to raise a child" is fully endorsed by most people. Thus, empowering them to use all of the support systems available to them is crucial to the treatment process. The use of these systems can be implemented at any stage in therapy, but the families must be aware of all potential systems before therapy is terminated so that they can readily tap into them if the need arises.

Unlike many treatment approaches, which are based on linear models, the Multi-CMS approach is based on the concept of circularity and is composed of four phases. Each component of each phase can recur repeatedly at various levels throughout treatment. The therapist must therefore be flexible and willing to intervene at whichever phase and whatever level in therapy. With this understanding, the flow of treatment for the Multi-CMS approach is outlined in detail below.

PHASE I. ASSESSMENT PROCESS

Step 1. Initial Assessment

The initial assessment stage, which occurs in the first therapy session, is broken into two phases: (a) explaining the process and (b) establishing trust (Chapter 4 discusses this assessment phase with respect to immigrant families). Because therapy is a relatively new phenomenon among many immigrants from "third-world" countries, and because most immigrants are taught to heal themselves within their own familial context, initially many immigrants are resistant to therapy. When immigrant families enter treatment, it is generally because they were referred by school personnel or child protective services due to difficulty with their children in school or due to charges of child abuse or inappropriate ways of disciplining their children. In an effort to establish a relationship, the therapist must clearly explain the therapeutic function, process clearing up any misconceptions, and explain the treatment process. Many do not understand how merely talking about one's problem can bring about relief and actual change. Also, many believe that therapy will be for only one session and that only the identified patient (in most cases, a child) will be involved. In fact, most families, especially those referred by child protective services for inappropriate discipline, do not believe they need therapy at all; as far as they are concerned, their forms of discipline are appropriate. To the therapist, this attitude may appear resistant, but from the clients' perspective, it is sensible if, in their countries of origin, corporal punishment is acceptable. Thus, it is important that the therapist not degrade the disciplinary measures they have used in the past, but rather explain alternatives. It is also necessary to explain that a therapist works with "normal, healthy" people who are simply experiencing adjustment difficulties, not just "crazy" people, as some tend to believe.

The next stage of this initial assessment process is the establishment of trust. This can be done through Sue's (1981) concepts of credibility and giving. According to Sue and Zane (1987), credibility refers to the client's perception of the therapist as a trustworthy and effective helper; credibility can be ascribed or achieved. Giving is the client's perception that something was gained from the therapeutic encounter. For most culturally diverse families, a therapist is more credible based on his or her ascribed status in keeping with cultural factors: age, gender, and education. In most societies around the world, the youth is subordinate to the elder, the female to the male, and the less educated individual to the more educated authority figure. A lack of ascribed credibility may be the main reason such clients resist therapy.

Credibility can also be achieved (instead of ascribed) based on the therapist's culturally relevant techniques, skills, and empathetic understanding. A lack of achieved credibility may be the reason clients terminate therapy prematurely. This is why the first session is so important in establishing credibility. Generally, clients will trust and view the therapist as more credible if he or she conceptualizes the client's problem in a manner consistent with the client's cultural experiences and beliefs. Thus, it may be more beneficial, for example, if the therapist appears understanding (though not necessarily supportive) of the parent's use of spanking. Conversely, a therapist who tells a child to be assertive to his or her parents may lose credibility.

It is important to remember that with this model, the assessment process (as is the therapeutic process) is ongoing and cyclic. Also, from the inception of therapy, the therapist using this model is engaging in problem solving by striving to alleviate clients' fears, misconceptions, and confusion within minutes of the first session.

Questions can include the following:

1. *Why are you here?* Given their response, therapists can help alleviate any guilt or anger via empathetic understanding. If their understanding of why they are there is different from that of the referral source, the therapist should mention the discrepancy only if it will not hurt the therapeutic alliance. If there is denial on the client's part, it can be addressed later in the session.
2. *Were you ever in therapy before?* If they were not, therapists should explain the therapeutic process.
3. *What are your thoughts about a psychotherapist or about psychotherapy?* Therapists should address their misconceptions or anger about being in therapy.

4. *What do you think you can gain from therapy?* In other words, what does the client want the therapist to address immediately? Addressing what the family views as most pressing will help to build the therapist's credibility as well as empower the family.

It might also be important to note:

1. The seating arrangement of family members: Who sits next to whom?
2. Who is the powerful figure in the family?
3. Who speaks on behalf of the family?
4. Are the children allowed to speak?
5. What significant family members are missing?

Step 2. Gathering Information

Therapists need to be aware that with most immigrants, copious note taking can be quite intimidating and distracting because families may feel the therapist is not paying attention. Thus, it is advised that note taking be kept to a minimum and the establishment of trust be the focus in the initial stage of treatment.

The genogram, a tool derived from anthropology but quite commonly used in psychology, is a sort of family tree. This can prove to be quite useful to the therapist working with culturally diverse families because of the many family members and friends who are directly or indirectly involved. If nothing else, it will allow the individual or family to visually represent their support systems. It can be equally beneficial simply to record the information without the use of a tree, using such questions as Who raised you? and Who did you live with prior to coming to the United States? Once a picture has been drawn, the therapist can encourage the family to bring in some or all of the family members who are impacting on the life of the identified patient.

Boyd-Franklin (1989) mentioned that information gathering on Black families often occurs later in the treatment process. She attributed this to the process of building trust, which must be established before extensive information gathering can take place. Whereas this may also be applicable to some immigrant families, most individuals want to get on with whatever is necessary so that they can be finished with therapy. Therefore, the therapist must determine whether the family is ready to engage in data collecting in the first session. It is important to keep in mind that with many immigrants, a therapist can establish credibility in the first few minutes of the first session merely by virtue of ascribed (professional) status.

Step 3. Determining the Stage of Acculturation

While it is important to keep in mind that not all families are in need of therapy because of acculturation stressors, with immigrant families, difficulties in acculturation can be a major contributing factor to their family problems. Determining if there is any transitional conflict via Helms's (1985) three stages of acculturation (preencounter stage, transitional stage, and transcendent stage) is important in helping immigrant families. A caveat, though: not all families are unable to negotiate the acculturation process. Some families need therapy for the same reasons Anglo-American families need therapy, for instance, the teenage rebellion typically found in any culture. In any event, once it has been determined which stage of acculturation the individual or family is in, it will be necessary to outline the goals for therapy based on the acculturation stage or any other transitional conflicts.

Step 4. Outlining the Goals

To further establish credibility, it is necessary, before the end of the first session, to outline concisely what the individual or family will gain; that is, the goals of therapy should be highlighted. This is to ensure that there is no discrepancy between the client's goals and the therapist's, since this can affect the therapist's credibility. As a matter of practice, at the end of every session, it is wise to reevaluate progress and see if the goals are being accomplished. Of course, even as the goals are being outlined, therapy can begin. Here again is a reminder that one advantage of this comprehensive model is that therapy can begin even while assessment is still in progress because of the cyclical nature of this treatment approach.

PHASE II. EDUCATIONAL TREATMENT PROCESS

In working with immigrant families, much of therapy may be educational in nature, since many adjustment difficulties may be due to cultural differences or a lack of knowledge about the host country's educational, social, and political systems. Gopaul-McNicol, Thomas, and Irish (1991) explore basic educational and social issues of which immigrant families need to be aware and the facilities that are available to help them in the process of adjustment. Understanding the American school system, particularly the special education process (a concept foreign to many immigrant families), was examined by Thomas and Gopaul-McNicol (1991). Gopaul-McNicol (1993) suggested that if, after the assessment process, it is determined that family members lack knowledge about these basic systems, which they have to deal with every day, they may have to be educated about these systems. This stage of therapy may also involve a lot of homework, such as reading (bibliotherapy), to gain an understanding of the various systems. As can be seen, effective therapy with immigrant families requires flexibility, the use of a circular model, and even the removal of some traditional rigid boundaries. Therapists must be willing to explore the impact of the educational, social, legal, political, and social conditions of the families they treat. To attempt to treat these families without addressing these systems could impair the therapist's credibility.

Regarding the legal system, the next treatment stage for clients who are in this country illegally is to educate and empower them. This may involve such things as helping them find an immigration attorney or explaining their rights with respect to their children's education. This means that the therapist must know the various systems, be willing to establish contact with the different providers in these systems, and, if necessary, include these providers in therapy sessions.

If the assessment shows that the child is embarrassed by the family (a problem many immigrant families face) because of the parents' accent, clothes, foods, and so forth, therapy has to focus on both the parents and the children. Parents generally feel rejected, frustrated, angry, and confused. In this stage, therapy has to focus on teaching parents the social-emotional adjustment stages that children go through. The goal of therapy is still educational at this point, because the therapist needs to assist the parents in understanding the following:

1. The causes of childhood misbehavior and the principles and concepts underlying the social learning of such behavior.
2. The cultural differences in values and discipline as they affect their children's adjustment.

3. The emotional stress and fears that emerge in a child as a result of migration and adjustment to a new family and the difference between an emotional disturbance and cultural adjustment.
4. The differences in the school structure; school expectations.
5. The criteria used by the school system in placing children in special programs, and parental rights.
6. How parents can build positive self-esteem and self-discipline in their children via a home study program, so that their children will be empowered to maintain a positive self-image in a race-conscious society.
7. How to communicate more effectively with their children and to be critical without affecting their child's self-esteem.
8. The impact of peer pressure and how it can be monitored.

At this juncture, therapy will be both educational and psychological, because the children ought to be taught the following:

1. To understand the sociocultural differences between their native country and the United States (educational).
2. To cope with peer taunts about their accents, mode of dressing, foods, family, and so forth (psychological).
3. To communicate more effectively with their families (educational and psychological).
4. To acquire the social skills and assertiveness skills needed (psychological).
5. To improve study skills and to understand cultural differences in test taking, school structure, school expectations, and language factors (educational).
6. To cope with the emotional stress and fears that come with migration (psychological).
7. To understand the psychology of being Black in American society (psychological).
8. To understand the concept of self-esteem, its relation to performance and success, and the sources, institutions, and images that affect self-esteem (educational and psychological).

If the assessment reveals that the child is in Helms's second stage, the transitional phase, the child realizes his or her lack of absolute acceptance by the White world. Individuals withdraw from the dominant culture and try to identify with their culture of origin and immerse themselves in the values and lifestyle of that culture. This is when many adolescents begin, for example, to wear dreadlocks, to rebel against their parents' Eurocentric view and talk emotionally of Mother Africa. In other words, they do not necessarily have a true understanding and a true appreciation of their history; they identify out of rebellion, due to a loss of culture, feelings of rejection, and a need to grasp anything left of their cultural pride. This is the most difficult stage for both parents and children. They all have to acknowledge racism and discrimination. The main affect is one of frustration and anger, and behavior is generally militant. Interpersonal relations tend to become limited mainly to one's own cultural group. Therapy has to be both extensive and intensive, tapping many modalities: affective, interpersonal, educational, behavioral, cognitive, structural, and many systems (individual, family, extended family, church, and community).

If the assessment shows that the child is in the final or transcendent stage of acculturation, the client may not need psychological therapy as such (at least, not for acculturation matters), because he or she has become bicultural and uses the experiences from both cultural groups to best fit his or her own circumstances.

PHASE III. PSYCHOLOGICAL TREATMENT PROCESS

The greater the cultural difference between therapist and client, the greater the challenge to maintain the relationship. These cultural differences can dominate the therapeutic relationship and affect therapeutic progress. The therapist's efforts to "cross over" may have to be greater with an immigrant family than with a family with similar values and customs as the therapist's. The combination of Lazarus's broad-base, multimodal approach, Minuchin's structural approach, and Bowen's family dynamics approach is the most helpful in addressing the psychological problems faced by immigrant families and in easing the "joining" or "crossing over" process. As has been demonstrated above, the initial stages of therapy with immigrant families tend to be solely educational, unless there is a crisis due to some traumatic incident. However, once the individual or family is familiar with the various systems, and if the problem persists (at times, therapy with immigrant families may be strictly educational), then a more psychological approach to treatment is needed.

Applying Multimodal Therapy with Immigrants

Multimodal assessment with its multilayered approach focuses on behaviors that are impeding the happiness and acculturation of immigrant families. The therapist will observe and ask what makes an individual sad, frightened, angry, anxious, timid, and so forth, as well as observe what type of behaviors the individual displays when feeling these emotions.

Generally, when maladaptive behaviors are present, traditional behavior therapy will be implemented. Thus, clients will be taught to practice prescribed exercises: relaxation, meditation, assertiveness training, modeling, and so forth. Behavioral contracts would be set up, whereby the client is rewarded for compliance and deprived of privileges for noncompliance. The works of behaviorists such as Skinner (1974), Bandura (1969), Wolpe (1969), Meinchenbaum (1977), and Jacobson (1938) can all be applied, depending on the nature of the problem.

As mentioned above, it is common in multimodal therapy to begin intervening in the first interview, rather than waiting until the full assessment procedure is completed, to alleviate stress. For example, if a child says he or she is stuttering because of feeling very nervous, Jacobson's (1983) progressive relaxation can be applied in the first session. In a sense, this will seem like a "gift" to the family, because a direct relationship between therapy and alleviation of problems will have been demonstrated. In other words, the family would have seen the gain immediately from the first session. The therapist's credibility will have been established as well.

There is a strong correlation among one's cognition, affect, and behaviors. How one feels (affect) to a large extent determines how one behaves and thinks; likewise, how one thinks influences how one feels and behaves. As a result, addressing the affective side by exploring feelings in an empathetic manner is recommended. Domokos-Cheng Ham, (1989a, 1989b) discusses how the therapist can "join" with immigrant families in an empathetic manner. Essentially, the author talks about the interactive process, the dyadic relationship between therapist and client, and the therapist's ability to convey emotional sensitivity. Gladstein (1983), Rogers (1975), and Asby (1975) all emphasized the value of the therapist's listening for feelings. As researchers and academicians, we have had a tendency to look for specificity; thus, when we encounter nonquantifiable elements, such as feelings and empathy, we attempt to dismiss them because these abstract constructs cannot be measured. We recommend that teaching a client to express affect is a process. Although it is important to proceed cautiously when attempting to uncover unconscious feelings, there is no doubt that culturally different families, when faced with their children's maladaptive behaviors, express some feelings very openly, in ways such as "I don't understand. This is not the way we behave. I feel frustrated. I am sending my child back home." What they are saying is that they cannot cope. Threatening to send the children back to their native land (after waiting so long to be reunited with them) is the ultimate expression of pain, fear, and anger. Therapy must address these feelings, as well as teach clients coping skills. The important factor to note here is that, while the therapist may be affectively empathetic, he or she must maintain "cognitive empathetic skills in perceiving, categorizing and making sense" of the client's feelings (Domokos-Cheng Ham, 1989a, p. 38). The idea, then, is not merely to feel what the client is feeling, but to comprehend and act on what the client is feeling. Affective therapy is best introduced somewhere around the middle to end phase of the therapeutic process. However, if the need arises earlier, the therapist should assist clients in amplifying their feelings.

Likewise, exploring how thoughts influence emotions and behavior, the therapist may try to examine clients' belief (cognition) systems. Examining clients' belief that their children "should, ought to, must" do well may help shed some light on the undue pressure that some parents place on their children, albeit unintentionally.

Albert Ellis's (1974) rational emotive therapy (RET), which is a cognitive, behavioral, and affective approach to treatment, is relevant to immigrant families for the following reasons:

1. It does not require clients to give up their values and cultural reality. Therefore, clients do not have to endorse the therapist's culture to get well. RET is a value-free form of therapy because it helps clients to achieve their goals within their own sociocultural context. Problems usually arise when clients' new belief system is in conflict with their cultural belief system. Thus, clients who no

longer share the views of their traditional culture may experience cognitive dissonance, which has to be worked through. In such a case, clients can be taught that it is not so "awful" if their goals or values have to be changed to function in this society. Similarly, clients can be taught that maintaining their traditional values is also acceptable.

2. It is proactive, short term, and goal-directed.
3. It provides clients with a link among their thoughts, affect, and behavior.
4. Rational beliefs are logical. Therefore, when a client believes, for instance, that coming to the United States has destroyed his manhood, he is made to recognize through RET that manhood is not so fragile a concept that any event can destroy it. Using this cognitive approach to therapy, many of a client's irrational thoughts can be examined. Therefore, parents who expect their children to like the cultural change merely because they did, or to do well because the opportunity is here, or to acculturate with minimal difficulty can benefit from RET.

Interpersonal relations is the area in which immigrant children experience the most difficulty in school. McNicol (1991) outlined, from a child's perspective, several areas of adjustment that children go through when they are reunited with their families. Many children fall at each end of the continuum—unassertiveness leading to withdrawal, or aggression leading to violence or disruptive behavior.

Teaching alternative ways of coping with problem situations via role play, assertiveness training, and social skills training should aid in addressing this problem. In addition, teaching children to cope with peer taunts and to understand the sociocultural differences between their native countries and the United States are some ways to improve their interpersonal relationships.

To improve self-esteem (a problem commonly seen) in immigrant children, it can be helpful to explore how they perceive themselves, their body, and self-image, with questions such as "What do you dislike or like about yourself?" and then observing how these images influence their moods, sensations, and behaviors. The child may persistently complain about unpleasant sensations, such as aches and pains; often, this is the child's way of communicating stress in dealing with the cultural transition. Cognitive-behavior therapy will address the child's anxieties, but parents also have to be taught how not to reinforce or cultivate the anxiety by allowing the child to skip school. Whenever immigrant parents come into conflict with the school system, an option they tend to consider is keeping the child out of school for a few days, hoping the problem will simply disappear when the child returns. Many of them are unaware of terms and realities such as educational neglect, and this must be taught to them. What can be seen in examining the multimodal approach to therapy is that when dealing with behavior, affect, sensation, imagery, cognition, and interpersonal factors, the emphasis is essentially educational. The therapist offers guidance, displays caring, modifies faulty styles, corrects misconceptions, provides information, and delivers the support necessary for clients to attain their goals.

In selecting which problems and which modality to address first, Lazarus (1976) recommends starting with the most obvious problem and using the most logical procedure. This will overcome the penchant for making straightforward problems needlessly complicated.

PHASE IV. EMPOWERMENT TREATMENT PROCESS

The empowering of the family via a multisystems approach is the final stage of treatment. Boyd-Franklin (1989) examines the importance of intervening at various levels—individual, family, extended family, place of worship, community, and social services. There is little doubt that this approach can be quite effective, because it provides a flexible set of guidelines for intervention with immigrant families. Encouraging individuals to embrace the support of their extended family and nonblood kin in areas such as child care and education may help in preventing personal difficulties. The use of the place of worship in therapy with immigrants is also very relevant, because of the importance religion plays in the life of most immigrant families. The place of worship can serve as a valuable social service in times of crisis, particularly for single parents. The therapist should suggest the place of worship as a support system and even seek permission from the family to talk to the priest or minister in attempting to ascertain what role it can play in the therapeutic process. Of course, it is also important for the therapist to recognize the significant influence of the folk beliefs in many religious societies. Leininger (1973) recommended using both in-digenous practitioner skills and professional practices. We do not be-lieve it is necessary for therapists to conduct spiritual counseling or to even have a referral list of folk practitioners, since one has to be knowl-edgeable to venture into this form of treatment and comfortable with this procedure to make such a referral. However, it is necessary for therapists to understand that their opposition to the family's seeking the help of such practitioners may impede the psychotherapeutic pro-cess. We have always provided emotional support to clients who felt they were victims of bewitchment and asked them to discuss what happened after their visits to spiritists.

Also critical is that the therapist must help the family find out what afterschool programs exist in their communities, since allegations of ne-glect are sometimes brought against working parents whose young chil-dren are at home alone after school. The families need to be taught that this is not accepted in American society and that child care programs can be used. Boyd-Franklin (1989) recommended that therapists should keep a file on these services so they can mobilize them when necessary. This kind of tapping of available resources is sometimes the single most important interaction in facilitating the possibility of treatment.

In addition, the therapist needs to be knowledgeable about the legal system as it applies to immigration policies and to be familiar with at least one immigration attorney because of the illegal immigration sta-tus of many immigrant families. The American Immigration Lawyers Association can provide a list of names from the individual's cultural background. Knowing about the immigration laws is important for therapists to be sensitive to the family's fears surrounding their immi-grant status and also to be able to help them with specific information, for example, that children cannot be denied a public education because of their immigrant status, a fact of which most culturally different families are unaware.

The Multi-CMS approach also recognizes that the idea that "it takes a whole community to raise a child" is fully endorsed by many people around the world. Immigrant families are generally not aware of the various systems (educational, legal, community), and empowering them to use all of the support systems available is crucial to the accul-turation process. The use of these systems can be implemented at any stage in therapy, but families must be aware of all potential systems before therapy is terminated so that they can readily tap into them if the need arises.

In general, in using the Multi-CMS approach to treating immigrant families, a therapist can explore a broad spectrum of techniques to address the needs of this population. The following is an example of how this comprehensive approach can be practically implemented.

CASE EXAMPLE

The Matthews family was referred for therapy by the school psychologist due to the academic and behavioral problems of their two sons, Michael and Kendall, ages 7 and 9, respectively. The eldest child, Taiesha, age 13, was also having academic difficulties, failing all courses except gymnastics. Mr. Matthews is originally from Jamaica and Mrs. Matthews from Trinidad and Tobago. They had met in Jamaica, where Mrs. Matthews spent two years after completing high school in Trinidad. They have been married for 14 years, although 8 years after they married, Mrs. Matthews emigrated to the United States "for a better life and to give my children the chance to get a good education." The children lived in Jamaica with their father and paternal grandparents. Michael was 1 year old when his mother left home, Kendall was 3, and Taiesha was 7. Because Mrs. Matthews had come to the United States on a holiday visa but had decided to stay on doing domestic work, she had lived for three years illegally in this country. In that time, she was unable to visit her children in Jamaica because she would not have been allowed reentry into the United States. She was later sponsored by her employer and obtained permanent residency (approximately five years after leaving home). She immediately sponsored her family, who are now here. Although they are not legal permanent residents yet, she expects them to become so within the next few months. When the family joined Mrs. Matthews, the children were then 6, 8, and 12. Currently, the household is composed of the nuclear family, a maternal aunt and uncle, and the maternal grandmother. The children have not seen the paternal grandparents with whom they lived since they left Jamaica.

These background data were sent by the school psychologist along with the referring information. In addition, there are allegations of possible child abuse and educational neglect due to the children's excessive absences from school. School officials are strongly considering placing both boys in special education due to emotional disturbances and Taiesha in special education due to a learning disability. However, they agreed to withhold special education placement until psychotherapeutic intervention occurred.

INITIAL SESSION

As had been agreed on the telephone, all members of the nuclear family came in for the first session. The therapist, having greeted the family, began the treatment process by asking the parents to discuss the problem as they understood it. Mrs. Matthews looked frustrated because Mr. Matthews was very angry that the family "had to be seen as crazy and abusive." He sat away from the rest of the family and did not say anything for the first 15 minutes. Mrs. Matthews explained much of what was mentioned in the referral, and the children were generally quiet. The therapist (who was a young, female clinical psychologist) initially found it necessary to address some of the family's misconceptions about the range of clients who seek counseling. The therapist also agreed with Mr. Matthews that many families are labeled abusive when in fact they are using culturally sanctioned ways of disciplining their children. At this juncture, Mr. Matthews "joined" with the therapist by sharing his frustration with this system. By conceptualizing the problem in a manner consistent with the family's cultural experiences and beliefs, the therapist gained credibility with Mr. Matthews. The therapist also used this session to enlighten the family about some basic social and cultural differences, such as sleeping arrangements, educational neglect, and the meaning of child abuse in American society. Sensitivity to the children's presence was taken into consideration, since the therapist wanted to respect the hierarchical order of family life structure and not reveal too much in the presence of the children. Both Mr. and Mrs. Matthews said at the end of the session how much they had learned about educational, social, and cultural differences. The therapist had given to the family a "gift," and the family had already seen the therapist as credible after the first session. The therapeutic process was explained, and the family agreed to give therapy a chance for at least one month.

Gathering Information and Outlining Goals

Both the first and the second sessions were spent gathering information as well as engaging in the treatment process. The Comprehensive Assessment Battery (Gopaul-McNicol, 1993) was used as a guide. The second session was quite enlightening, and several issues were revealed as problems within the family:

1. Mr. Matthews's unemployment.
2. The children's feeling that they did not belong in the school and that their parents did not understand them.
3. Taiesha's embarrassment about her parents' accent and cultural values.
4. The maternal grandmother's attitude toward her son-in-law because her daughter was now the breadwinner (working two jobs).
5. The spanking of all the children by extended family members.
6. The parents' belief that Taiesha "had gotten rude."
7. The endorsement of the folk belief that "it is possible someone in Jamaica envied us because they heard we were doing well and put something [a hex] on the children."
8. The fear that the children "will be deported home if they continue to give trouble in school."

The therapist continued to engage in the treatment process by explaining the educational and legal rights of the family. At the end of the session, the family was also given homework: reading two handbooks for immigrants on the educational and social systems and on special education. At the end of this session, some goals were outlined, which included empowering the family to use the educational support systems in their communities to help the children in math and reading. The therapist also supported the family's decision to visit a spiritist by asking to be kept abreast of the results of their meetings with the obeah practitioner. In the meantime (during session interim), the therapist sent a letter to the school explaining to the principal that supplemental instruction in English language (SIEL) might prove to be beneficial for all of the children. Goals also involved teaching all adults in the household alternative ways of disciplining children, as well as examining the effect of family role change on the family's stability.

EMPOWERMENT THROUGH THE EXTENDED FAMILY AND THE
IMPLEMENTATION OF THE EDUCATIONAL AND PSYCHOLOGICAL
TREATMENT PROCESSES

There was much resistance from members of the extended family to coming in for treatment because they did not think that the problems with the children were caused by them. Therefore, the therapist suggested making a home visit; thus, the third session of family therapy was conducted at home. As agreed, the entire family was at home upon the therapist's arrival. The family was more responsive to therapy being conducted in the home. In addressing the resistance, the therapist did not agree or disagree with the extended family's attitude that they did not need therapy but rather spoke of contributions family members could make in helping to solve the problem. Resistance was diminished considerably, in that each family member explored ways he or she could be of more assistance. The aunt and uncle agreed to help in the areas of remediation and in spending more time with the children. This session also focused briefly on what constitutes child abuse. Extended family members recognized that they had been unaware of the legal ramifications of engaging in corporal punishment. Subsequent sessions with the adults were also educational in nature, in that the focus was on the emotional stress that children experience as a result of immigration and their concomitant shift in value orientation. The differences in the school structure and expectations, test-taking styles, and so forth were all examined.

By this time, the family had agreed to continue with therapy for another month, and the extended family members had agreed to come into the clinic. At this juncture, both family and group therapy were being provided on a weekly basis. From the fourth session up to the end of therapy, Michael and Kendall joined a group for young boys, while Taiesha joined a group for teenage girls. In both groups, issues such as coping with peer pressure, social skills and assertiveness training (to assist with interpersonal relations), building self-esteem, understanding the educational differences in test-taking styles, and coping with their fears about acculturation were addressed. In addition, Michael and Kendall were taught self-control separate from the group, while Taiesha's embarrassment around her parents' accent and her father's refusal to treat her as a teenager were discussed in a family session.

Family therapy was held with the adults only to address the conflict as a result of family role changes. The children were asked to sit outside when marital issues were being discussed. Mr. and Mrs. Matthews both felt uncomfortable that having the children sit in on the therapy session would result in their knowing about marital conflicts. This wish was respected, but Mrs. Matthews's mother, who was also a catalyst in creating stress on Mr. Matthews, was expected to be in attendance. Rational emotive therapy explored their cultural beliefs about men being the sole breadwinners. In addition, the role conflict for children and parents was addressed in family therapy by helping family members to establish some individuation, but at the same time maintaining family cohesiveness. Group therapy for Taiesha also addressed how adolescents can prepare their families at each stage of the differentiation process. Furthermore, group therapy focused on helping Taiesha to understand her parents' perception of the hierarchies within the family and what this means in relation to respect.

In addition, the family was taught the principles of behaviorism and how they may have directly or indirectly reinforced negative behaviors in one another. A behavior modification program was set up at home, whereby the children were reinforced for good behavior and effort in school. After obtaining the parents' informed consent, the teachers were sent letters explaining what was being done and how it would be helpful for them to send home the daily behavior checklist so that the family could appropriately reward the children. The children were then further rewarded by the therapist during group therapy time.

It was not until the sixth family session that the children's not feeling loved by their family was addressed. The children's feelings about their father's "abuses" and their mother's extended hours at work were also discussed. Kendall was particularly emotional as he talked about not feeling loved because his father never hugged him. This session focused on touching as a form of communicating, and everyone was asked to hug the person nearest him or her. Then all were told to hug whichever family members they so desired. Interestingly, no one reached to hug Mr. Matthews until it was pointed out by the therapist. At that point, he said he would like to hug everyone and proceeded to do so. From that session onward, homework involved daily, tactile forms of communication. In the meantime, the reality of Mrs. Matthews needing to work to pay the bills was explored, but all family members decided they would assist in domestic matters so that she would be free to engage in family activities once she got home. Mr. Matthews, who before had refused to cook, agreed to do so, so that Mrs. Matthews would not have to get up early to cook before leaving for work. In addition, Mr. Matthews agreed to enroll in an educational program to obtain his high school diploma while still seeking employment.

The ninth session in treatment was again educational, and family members were encouraged to establish contact with more social support systems. Taiesha joined a youth group that was monitored by West Indian adults in the community. She built a wonderful network of friends who themselves had gone through cultural conflicts while in transition. Mr. Matthews eventually agreed to join a Black male self-esteem group, which focused on such issues as "the invisibility syndrome" as it pertains to Black males and the psychology of being a Black male in this society. All family members agreed to become members of their local church. The therapist established contact with the pastor, who introduced the family to the congregation at Mass.

In the meantime, the children continued to show academic delays, but behavior problems had decreased considerably. The therapist visited the school with the parents and suggested at a school-based support-team (SBST) meeting what each discipline (psychologist, nurse, social worker, teacher) could be responsible for in assisting these children. This was a difficult task, given the bureaucracy in the education system, but they did agree to refrain from placing the children in special education for at least two years.

The success of this case may be a result of the holistic approach to therapy. The Multi-CMS approach, although demanding, covered all areas that caused distress within the family unit. In addition, the concept "it takes a whole community to raise a child" certainly aided this family in arming and empowering themselves as they attempted to acculturate to American society.

PART FOUR

ISSUES IN CROSS-CULTURAL TRAINING

CHAPTER 7

Creating Multicultural Teaching-Training Programs

THE HISTORY OF CROSS-CULTURAL TEACHING AND TRAINING

OVER THE PAST 25 years, a number of events have come together to bring us to the current status of cross-cultural teaching. At some point there was increased awareness of the growing ethnic minority population in the United States. As more and more psychologists were faced with numbers of these ethnic groups in their clinical work, some psychologists recognized the ethical dilemma posed by continuing to serve these people without adequate preparation (Bernal & Castro, 1994; Cayleff, 1986). In 1973, a conference sponsored by the American Psychological Association was held in Vail, Colorado, with the goal of addressing some of these issues (Korman, 1976). Then in 1979, the education and training committee of Division 17 of the APA met to outline what they considered to be the minimum competencies for training counselors working in cross-cultural situations (Bernal & Castro, 1994). Since then, the field of counseling psychology has been a leader in the efforts of psychologists to provide fair and good assessment, treatment, and consultation to ethnic minorities. Clinical psychology put forth a similar effort, but only 20% of the clinical programs had a cross-cultural course in 1982 (Bernal & Castro, 1982; Mio, 1989).

WHAT SHOULD THE STUDENT KNOW ABOUT CROSS-CULTURAL ISSUES?

The following outline from Sue (1981) explicates the training goals of cross-cultural competency for psychologists:

I. Attitudinal competencies
   A. Psychologist is knowledgeable about his or her own ethnic heritage.
   B. Psychologist is aware of his or her own biases.
   C. Psychologist has developed a level of comfort with ethnic differences.
   D. Psychologist knows when it is appropriate to make a referral to a psychologist of the same ethnic background as the client (Midgette & Meggert, 1991).
II. Knowledge competencies
   A. Psychologist understands the sociology of minority groups.
   B. Psychologist has the necessary cultural knowledge about his or her client.
   C. Psychologist has basic therapeutic/counseling skills.
   D. Psychologist is aware of institutional barriers to minority clients.
III. Skill competencies
   A. Psychologist is able to choose and implement appropriate and effective interventions with minority clients (Midgette & Meggert, 1991).

FORMAT OF THE COURSE

There is an ongoing discussion about the best way to teach cross-cultural material. Copeland (1982) lists four didactic approaches: a separate course, an area of concentration, an interdisciplinary approach, and an integration model.

The most frequently found didactic approach is the single course (Copeland, 1982; Reynolds, 1995). This method has been criticized for (a) its lack of depth; (b) the high probability that such a superficial glimpse of the lives and values of certain ethnic minority groups will only lead to further stereotyping; and (c) the absence of any integration of what is learned about certain ethnic groups and what the student should do with that knowledge in therapeutic, testing, or consultation situations (Reynolds, 1995). The current reply to this last criticism is the recommendation that every course in the graduate curriculum be taught with attention to cross-cultural issues.

A second debate has to do with whether the course should be didactic or process-oriented. A course that is completely didactic places all of the information to be processed on an intellectual level. In contrast, a process orientation encourages students to examine their own feelings, values, and biases and how these might influence the cross-cultural therapeutic meeting.

INSTITUTIONAL BARRIERS TO THE FORMATION OF CROSS-CULTURAL COURSES

At the very core of all obstacles to the inclusion of cross-cultural material in clinical and counseling graduate programs lies the issue of whether this area is seen as a relevant and necessary part of clinical training. Many professors would not think to teach this material because it was not a part of their own graduate training. Other professors, adopting a less benign attitude, believe that what is already taught in most graduate programs across the country (about theories of psychopathology, assessment, and treatment) is more than adequate because of their belief in the applicability of these theories to all patients regardless of race or ethnicity.

The APA accrediting body in more recent years has prevailed upon departments to have at least one cross-cultural course. However, some barriers in accomplishing this were noted. First, where was the funding coming from for such a course, and second, once funding was secured, who would teach it (Reynolds, 1995)? In most cases, there was no one on the faculty with the desire or appropriate background to do the teaching. This meant that a faculty member had to be recruited. According to Reynolds (1995), ineffective strategies have been utilized to get these minority faculty members on board. The lack of effectiveness can be attributed at least in part to (a) too heavy a reliance on word-of-mouth candidates recommended by the present faculty, (b) a reluctance to spend money on advertising, and (c) a reluctance to take the search beyond mainstream organizations and reach out to minority professional organizations.

Additional barriers arise even when a handful of suitable minority candidates are acquired. These candidates are sometimes met with particularly grueling interview processes, often being asked to submit materials or do things majority candidates have not been asked to do. If the process gets as far as making the candidate an offer, sometimes that offer is not reflective of the candidate's experience and level of expertise. Some departments respond to APA site visitors' queries by stating that either there were no suitable candidates to be found or that they interviewed and offered the job to someone but were turned down. The poor results of ineffective recruitment strategies have kept accrediting agencies at bay for years. When that explanation has been used for too long, however, the department eventually has to hire someone or risk being put on probation by the accrediting body.

The challenge of installing this cross-cultural material into the curriculum is not over once a minority faculty member is hired. The course curriculum has to be approved and there has to be adequate enrollment in the class. When classes like this are optional, many students do not sign up for it, taking the position that they will not be working with ethnic minority populations once their training is over. Other students believe that *ethnic minority* is synonymous with *poor* and again believe that their practices postdegree will be with a fairly homogeneous middle- or upper-middle-class group.

Reynolds (1995) points out a special issue for the minority professor and the students taking the course: the way this subject matter, and the people who are studying it, are treated by other faculty members. Is cross-cultural work seen as important? Are students encouraged to do research in this area? Are professors encouraged to do their own research in this area? If they are verbally supported by the department, what kind of financial, technical, and staff support is offered? Are the journals where cross-cultural articles are being published viewed as acceptable, quality journals? Is there any support for increasing the entire department's exposure to diversity issues, such as examining the needs of the population being served by the department clinic, bringing in speakers to give colloquiums and having the funds to remunerate them? The answers to these questions serve as a rough barometer of department attitudes.

ISSUES FOR PROFESSORS

BUREAUCRATIC PROCEDURES

In this section, the authors would like to go over some of the many problems facing the professor who is assigned or who volunteers to teach such a course. Most university settings have some procedure in place to assign a new course a number. This number allows students to indicate their course preferences on registration forms. Often, before that number can be assigned, the professor must prepare a course syllabus that will be submitted to and reviewed by a departmental curriculum committee. The format for syllabi differ from university to university as well as from department to department within a university. In general, the following information is included: a statement of the rationale for the course, the goals and objectives of the course, a description of how those goals and objectives are going to be met, course requirements, a bibliography, and the method for arriving at grades.

A very interesting question arises at this stage, namely, who on the curriculum committee is in a position to evaluate such a submission. The fact that these types of courses have never been taught before coupled with the fact that most professors, particularly the more senior ones, have not been exposed to this material in their own training suggests that there isn't anyone on staff to determine the appropriateness or exhaustiveness of the course syllabus as it has been prepared. This acceptance or rejection is the first obstacle the professor has to face.

TEACHING MINORITY STUDENTS

Once the course has been approved, assigned a number, and has adequate enrollment, the professor must then deal with the student body. The transferential reactions of students to the professor and to the course itself can run the gamut. Minority professors may find themselves being challenged by students who on some level have accepted a stereotype about the intellectual capabilities of people belonging to that minority group. This challenging behavior can take the form of questioning the credentials of the professor. On the other hand, minority students in the class, excited about having a mentor/role model, may idealize the minority professor. Majority students may also idealize the professor but for different reasons; they may be eager to ward off conflict and mistrust by demonstrating to the minority professor their lack of prejudice.

But minority professors are not the only vulnerable instructors of these courses. White professors must deal with the possibility of not being accepted by minority students, who may feel that the professor does not possess the requisite knowledge and expertise in this subject.

Another issue for White professors involves how to handle minority students who participate very little in class. Again, a society that values self-disclosure never quite understands or accepts the silent member. This is not to say that the only reason a minority student could have for not fully participating in class is related to his or her cultural values regarding sharing. In many instances, minority students are very eager to make their contribution but fear being ridiculed and ostracized by the rest of the class.

The following examples illustrate how minority students' experiences in class can mirror their experiences in the larger society. It is therefore incumbent upon the professor, minority or majority, to be cognizant of the ethnic composition of the class to be sure that individual minority students do not get scapegoated.

Case Example

Conchatta was a 26-year-old graduate student in a Ph.D. clinical psychology program at a major Catholic university. She originally came from Brazil, having gone through grade school and some college there. She came to the United States to complete her bachelor's degree and pursue her Ph.D.

Conchatta was the only student of Latin descent in the multicultural course offered by the department. Every time she spoke, her classmates snickered or rolled their eyes in a gesture of exasperation. On occasions when Conchatta would say something that one of her classmates did not agree with, her English would be criticized, she would be lectured to about her supposed lack of understanding of what goes on in America, or she would get an unsolicited interpretation of what she truly meant to say.

After this had happened several times, Conchatta stopped participating. She showed up on time for class and assiduously took notes and turned in assignments, but she no longer participated in discussions.

Case Example

A young African American male student was constantly criticized by his White classmates for bringing up the issue of the enslavement of Blacks by Whites. Many said it was water under the bridge and suggested that this history had little to do with the current situations with African Americans in this country.

TEACHING NONMINORITY STUDENTS

A much overlooked factor in these classroom situations is the emotional life of the professor. How does the minority professor deal with his or her feelings when students make comments that are offensive about the group to which the professor belongs? Can the professor separate the student's opinions from the student's grasp of the knowledge? A student's getting under the skin of the professor is not a new phenomenon. Traditionally, university professors have had an outlet for their feelings and a forum where they could get feedback from fellow professors; sometimes the feedback was in the form of relating similar or dissimilar experiences with the same students. What is different here is that often minority professors do not have peers (other minority professors) within their own departments to discuss these issues with and garner support.

At the other end of the continuum are the students who go to great lengths not to offend the minority professor.

Case Example

The students in a multicultural course being taught by a Latino professor were given the assignment of writing a short paper about their non-clinical experiences with minority people. They were to include some statement about where they obtained most of their information about minorities. Another part of the assignment required them to discuss what they learned about minorities from their families. Who was considered a minority by family members? What were they told about those groups of people? What level of interaction was permissible? In other words, did they live in neighborhoods where some minority people lived? Could they play with minority children? Could they go to the homes of minority children? Were they familiar with minorities only in the context of being servants to their family? Could they date minority people?

One young White male in the class approached the professor in private before turning in his paper. He said that he was very embarrassed about the way his father had referred to Hispanic or Latin people, calling them *Spics*. In his paper he described growing up in this atmosphere and mentioned the terminology his father so frequently used. The student wanted to know if he should leave the word *Spic* in the paper because he did not want to hurt the professor's feelings.

CURRICULUM

It is clear from reading the literature that there is no consensus about the most effective way to teach cross-cultural material (Copeland, 1982). Offering a single course may or may not be the best method, but at this time it is the way most often chosen to convey the material (Reynolds, 1995). The authors have found the following topics to constitute important parts of the course syllabus:

1. *Definition of terms* that the professor will be using throughout the course. *Culture, race, ethnicity, bias, prejudice,* and *discrimination* are just some examples of terms that need clarification.

2. *Majority and minority:* the authors have had the experience of teaching a class in which each student believed that his or her ethnic group was a minority in the United States. Essentially, their position was that pretty much every group was a minority. Interestingly, the one group that many students believed constituted the majority we were discussing was White Anglo-Saxon Protestants. Many professors choose to define the parameters of their courses around ethnic minority groups of color. An understandable and very strong argument for this is that the members of these groups have experienced a great deal of racism and discrimination because of their visibility as targets. However, there are other subgroups whose skin color is white who constitute an ethnic minority in this country and who have experienced racism, namely, the Jewish people. The professor not only has to decide on how to define *majority* and *minority* but also how to define *culture*. Some would argue that women and members of the gay and

lesbian populations are minorities in this country, with a culture of their own. For this reason, many courses on cross-cultural issues have included lectures devoted to gender bias and heterosexual bias in psychotherapy and counseling. However the parameters are drawn, it is essential that the professor make this clear at the beginning of class and be open to questions about how the decision was made to include or exclude certain groups.

3. *A delineation of the values* embedded in our therapeutic theories and interventions. It has been our experience that many students are surprised by this information, as they have always assumed that psychotherapy is one of the most value-free and nonjudgmental processes one can engage in.

4. *Discussion* of how these values are most closely shared with the majority culture.

5. *The influence of culture* on help-seeking behavior. The professor can discuss the ways in which culture is one of the factors that dictates what an individual considers to be a problem, how an individual manifests distress, when an individual will go for help, where or from whom an individual seeks help, and what an individual believes to be helpful (McGoldrick, Pearce, & Giordano, 1982).

6. *Cultural values,* help-seeking behavior, and the attitudes toward mental illness and psychological care of ethnic groups of color: Black Americans, Latin Americans, Asian Americans, and Native Americans.

7. *The use of translators* in clinical situations.

8. *Handling racism* in the session.

9. *Cross-cultural assessment.*

10. *Cross-cultural research methodology.*

11. *Ethics:* issues associated with not being adequately prepared to work with ethnic minorities.

RECOMMENDATIONS FOR A PILOT CROSS-CULTURAL
TRAINING PROGRAM (4 SEMESTERS)

Semester 1

The first semester is focused on the second criteria of Sue's (1981) outline: knowledge acquisition. This semester-long course would familiarize the student with the cultural values of various ethnic minority groups, how those values might depart from majority-held worldviews, what experiences these groups have had in their native countries or in the United States that have shaped their attitudes about prejudice and racism, what their attitudes are toward illness in general and mental illness in particular, what culture-bound syndromes (if any) exist, to what extent members of these groups are under- or overdiagnosed by majority culture nosology, and what are their expectations for help.

Semester 2

This would be required by anyone taking the cross-cultural sequence and would be composed of the students from the first semester. The goal of this semester is to help students get in touch with their own culture and possible biases and to help them identify their motivations for working with these ethnic populations. It is expected that the level of self-disclosure for this type of self-examination is not going to be present in the first semester of this class. Asking students to look at their own biases in a one-semester course is frequently met with defensiveness and denial. It is hoped that there will be some level of comfort established after the students have been together for an entire semester.

Practicum

The limited empirical literature advocates some experiential component to the cross-cultural training package (Mio, 1989). Each student would be required to carry a psychotherapy case in which the client is an ethnic minority. This practicum would take place during the second semester. The student would have individual and group supervision.

Semester 3

This semester focuses on the current status of cross-cultural research, learning how to critique the strengths and weaknesses of the present literature, learning about research methods particularly useful in this area, and identifying areas in need of empirical attention.

Semester 4

This course is for those students who are interested in pursuing research projects in the cross-cultural area.

In addition, throughout the program, assessment sequences already a part of the curriculum can be modified to address the use of the instruments with ethnic minorities; psychotherapy courses (regardless of orientation) can be added to address cross-cultural therapeutic dyad issues; and support group for faculty and peer support group for students should be established to provide opportunities for academic and emotional feedback.

CHAPTER 8

Training in Cross-Cultural Supervision

C LINICAL SUPERVISION can be defined as a process by which senior psychologists provide oversight for the work of junior psychologists or the work of other psychologists who wish to gain expertise in a specific area. This process of supervision involves constructing a bridge between what the supervisee has learned in didactic course work and what he or she needs to do in the room with actual psychotherapy clients.

Although there is a substantial body of literature on supervision and a growing body of literature on cross-cultural issues in counseling and psychotherapy, comparatively little has been written about the impact of racial, cultural, and ethnic differences between supervisor and supervisee on the supervisory process (Brown & Landrum-Brown, 1995; Leong & Wagner, 1994; Remington & DaCosta, 1989). The goals of the first part of this chapter are to discuss the characteristics of the supervisory relationship, to discuss the ways interethnic supervision can be different from similar-ethnic supervision, to examine how cross-cultural issues can influence supervision, and to provide recommendations that will facilitate an increase in the sensitivity of individual supervisors and institutions.

Before proceeding any further it should be noted that the authors are not unaware of the third party in all of this, namely, the client. Brown and Landrum-Brown (1995) have outlined the importance of considering all three parties in any discussion of supervision. Whenever appropriate, we will attempt to point out what the client may experience as a result of unresolved problems in the supervisory dyad.

THE SUPERVISORY RELATIONSHIP

The basic supervisory relationship usually consists of two people: the supervisor and the supervisee. In the case of group supervision, there is one supervisor and multiple supervisees. This relationship is one of unequal power, with the supervisor, more often than not, having the lion's share of power. This inequality is manifested in a variety of ways. Supervisors usually decide the time, place, length, and frequency of supervision. They usually set the ground rules regarding what should take place in the session (a review of videotapes, audiotapes, process notes, etc.). In some instances, the number and type of cases assigned to the supervisee are decided by the supervisor.

Another aspect of supervision is the uneven level of self-disclosure between the two parties. Certainly, there is some variation among individuals, but for the most part, supervisors tend not to reveal personal information about themselves. Psychology trainees may reveal more than they want to about themselves because of a sense that this is what is expected and that to fail to do so would meet with disapproval from the supervisor. In addition, some trainees, because of their novice status, may not know where to draw the line between appropriate disclosure for supervisory purposes (i.e., clarifying countertransferential issues) and the disclosure of material that is better discussed in one's own therapy. It is clear that supervisees can find themselves in a vulnerable position.

Another potential area of disclosure has to do with the history of one's clinical triumphs and failures. The very nature of supervision, with its training component, suggests that the supervisee has something to learn. The process of supervision involves bringing in samples of what the therapist did in therapy with the client and offering it to the supervisor for commentary. Supervisors fall anywhere along a continuum of willingness to expose their actual clinical skills. One supervisor might encourage supervisees to view him or her conducting a live session. Another supervisor might enthusiastically include his or her own audio/videotapes as part of supervision. There are others who will talk about their clinical mistakes. The more the supervisor shares, the more he or she does to equalize some of the power in the relationship. This type of sharing also accomplishes other things: it has the potential to normalize supervisees' feelings about how they handled a situation, and it sends the message to the supervisee that it is all right to make mistakes.

This brings us to what is probably the most salient feature of supervision (particularly for the supervisee): the evaluation component. No matter how collegial supervisors attempt to make the relationship, there is still the specter of evaluation hanging in the air. The knowledge that the supervisee has of the supervisor's power to criticize, praise, or be indifferent will certainly influence his or her decisions and actions.

INTERETHNIC, RACIAL, OR CULTURAL SUPERVISION

It has been suggested that the supervisory relationship described above has very strong parallels with the therapeutic relationship (Cook, 1994). If one accepts this premise, it would stand to reason that the very same issues that influence the cross-cultural therapeutic dyad have the potential to influence the cross-cultural supervisory dyad.

MINORITY SUPERVISEE AND MAJORITY SUPERVISOR

It has already been pointed out that minority clients in cross-cultural therapeutic dyads may bring with them to therapy expectations that reflect the treatment they have received or been exposed to in the larger society (Davis & Proctor, 1989). If the minority supervisee–majority supervisor dyad is analogous to the therapeutic one, then similar dynamics will be present. One manifestation of how these two dyads mirror the relationship between ethnic minorities and members of the majority in our society is reflected in the power imbalance between supervisor and supervisee. Pinderhughes (1989) has outlined and stressed the importance of examining the power dynamic to be effective in clinical work. Whereas all supervisees are in a subordinate position, those supervisees who are members of the majority may find this an atypical experience or simply proceed with the knowledge that once they leave supervision, they will go out to a world in which they are privileged.

The impact of the power differential on minority supervisees is varied and diffuse. It can result in the supervisee's limiting disclosure of personal material (even when appropriate) in supervision for fear that the information will be used against him or her. For many minorities, particularly the visible ones, a certain level of guardedness and a minimal level of disclosure have been tools of survival (Grier & Cobbs, 1968).

Minority supervisees may also experience high levels of anxiety as they worry about being negatively evaluated by their majority supervisors on the basis of racial and ethnic stereotypes rather than their performance (McNeill, Hom, & Perez, 1995). Such levels of anxiety in some minority supervisees can lead to hesitancy about revealing any flaws to the supervisor, for example, a reluctance to play video or audiotapes or a failure to relate problematic portions of a therapy session.

Another issue relates to the differing worldviews that supervisor and supervisee might have (Brown & Landrum-Brown, 1995). What happens when minority supervisees discover aspects of traditional psychological theory that are at odds with their cultural values? Can these issues be raised by the supervisee, and if they are brought up in supervision, what are the consequences? What can a minority supervisee do with a supervisor who is overtly or covertly racist? An empirical study conducted by McRoy, Freeman, Logan, and Blackmon (1986) confirmed that minority supervisees were concerned about all of the above-mentioned situations. Obviously, further research needs to be done to establish how these supervisees handled those situations and which methods were most successful.

But what about the barriers to effective supervision that can be brought into the relationship by the majority supervisor? A lack of understanding on the part of the supervisor of the worldview and value system of the supervisee can lead to gross misunderstandings about what is supposed to go on in the supervision hour. A common manifestation of these misunderstandings can be found in a misinterpretation of the behavior of the supervisee. For example, the supervisee who comes from a culture where one demonstrates respect for one's superiors by talking very little and listening a lot may be seen by a supervisor as passive and lacking in motivation or initiative.

Another barrier is the conscious or unconscious prejudice of the supervisor. When a supervisor chooses to believe all of the negative stereotypes about a group regarding their intelligence, industriousness, and psychological mindedness, there are consequences. In the extreme, this can lead to apathy about the training experience the supervisee has. There can be a reluctance to teach psychotherapy. The supervisor may then assign a caseload of mostly chronic, mentally ill patients who require lots of case management and do not afford the supervisee an opportunity to engage in psychotherapy. Or the supervisee may be assigned only minority clients whom the supervisor believes to be as lacking in psychological savvy as the supervisee (Remington & Da-Costa, 1989). But probably the most important fallout from prejudicial attitudes is the comparison of minority supervisees to White supervisee's and the creation of different standards for the minority supervisee. A frequent example of this is when a particularly difficult case is assigned to the minority supervisee; if the supervisee has trouble with the case, the supervisor may take this as evidence of the limited talents of members of the supervisee's ethnic group, disregarding the fact that anyone who had been assigned the same case would have had difficulty (Remington & DaCosta, 1989).

At the other end of the spectrum, problems in the cross-cultural supervisory relationship can be created by majority supervisors who circumvent the issue of race and/or adopt a stance of color blindness (Remington & DaCosta, 1989). The motivation for this stance is not consistent across all supervisors who adopt it. For example, some supervisors may take the position because their own professional training did not discuss cross-cultural issues; or, because race, ethnicity and culture were not thought to be factors affecting therapy and supervision, supervisors may see no need to address them (Remington & DaCosta, 1989). Other supervisors may simply be afraid to bring up racial issues because they do not know what to do once they are brought up or because of the anxiety they have about the reaction of their supervisees.

Finally, there is what Remington and DaCosta (1989) refer to as the reaction formation of majority supervisors. Not wanting to appear or be labeled in any way racist, these supervisors go to great lengths not to criticize or offend minority supervisees. Unfortunately, minority supervisees suffer because of it: (a) they may not get the accurate feedback necessary to improve and consolidate their therapeutic skills; (b) they may have to deal with the angry reactions of White peers who interpret this as preferential treatment (Remington & DaCosta, 1989); and (c) they may not learn anything about how to handle differences of opinion with a supervisor, which is vital to their continuing role as an apprentice.

MINORITY SUPERVISOR AND MAJORITY SUPERVISEE

The growing pressure on graduate programs in psychology to recruit and hire minority faculty has increased the number of minority supervisor–majority supervisee dyads in academia. This number can be added to the cross-cultural supervisory dyads that already exist in urban clinics, community mental health centers, and hospitals, where a vast majority of minority clinical psychologists choose to practice and where a large number of majority students end up doing their externships and internships. However, the suggestion that there is an increase in the minority supervisor–majority supervisee dyad is in no way an indication that it is equal in number to the previously discussed dyad. The number of minority clinical psychologists continues to lag substantially behind the number of majority clinical psychologists. And, because there are so few minority supervisors, the literature has virtually ignored the problems they have to face.

The uniqueness of this relationship lies in the fact that it goes against the societal norm for relationships between majority and minority people, namely, that the majority person is in the powerful and entitled position and the minority person is marginalized and less powerful. Remington and DaCosta (1989) have outlined the key issues in such a relationship: (a) majority supervisees may be confused due to a lack of familiarity in dealing with minority people in positions of authority; (b) some majority supervisees may rebel against the supervisor; this rebellion may take the form of disrespect, not seeing the supervisor as an expert, ignoring suggestions made by the supervisor, seeking out majority supervisors to get supplemental supervision, questioning the credentials of the supervisor, being combative and uncooperative, and/or giving the minority supervisor poor ratings; (c) when the client is a member of the majority and makes bigoted statements, supervisees may emphasize these statements in supervision as a way of passive-aggressively acting out their own biases toward supervisors, or the supervisee could be protective of the supervisor and omit these statements from a recounting of the session; and (d) when the client is a member of the same minority group as the supervisor, supervisees may omit what they perceive as negative information about the client for fear that they will be seen by the minority supervisor as bigoted.

All of the items mentioned by Remington and DaCosta (1989) are examples of reaction formation or confrontation and hostility. Any one of them jeopardizes the effectiveness of clinical supervision and, in turn, the care of the client.

We have painted some of the issues in cross-cultural supervision in broad, monochromatic, and possibly unidimensional strokes; Brown and Landrum-Brown (1995) have done an excellent job of refining this picture and rendering it in a more three-dimensional style. First, they talk about the fact that although we are dealing with a supervisory dyad, that dyad cannot be considered in isolation of the triangle of which it is a part: namely supervisor, supervisee, and client. Second, they have identified three dimensions relevant to the triangle: "differences from the general population, differences from one's cultural group, and differences from either or both of the other parties in the supervisory process" (p. 266). In fact, the second dimension, differences from one's own cultural group, has been addressed by Cook (1994). Expanding upon the work of Helms (1985, 1992) on Racial Identity Models for People of Color and for Whites, Cook suggests that if we accept the idea that individuals within one racial category do not have one homogeneous racial identity, then it stands to reason that the people involved in the supervisory relationship have to be examined at levels beyond the dichotomous categorizations of majority/minority, Black/White, European/non-European, and so forth.

MODELS OF SUPERVISION

Leong and Wagner (1994) reviewed the literature on cross-cultural supervision; as part of that review, they examined existing models of cross-cultural supervision. In their critique, the overwhelming criticism of all the models was the absence of any empirical research to buttress their assertions. Many models failed to provide specifics about how to increase the supervisee's level of cultural awareness or how to increase the awareness level of the supervisor. Because not all supervisees enter supervision at the same level (in other words, not all supervisees are beginners), Leong and Wagner thought that developmental changes in the supervisee should be taken into consideration in any model. Some of the models focused exclusively on the supervisee-client stem of the supervisory triangle, ignoring conscious or unconscious dynamics of the supervisor-supervisee stem. Other models were limited in their generalizability because they spoke exclusively about the Black/White racial dyad.

Although the Leong and Wagner (1994) review was extensive, there seemed to be a heavier emphasis on limitations, and very little was said about strengths.

The authors have found the schemata in Figure 8.1 helpful in our work with supervisees. We view the supervisory relationship as a sociopolitical structure. In other words, we are always taking into consideration how gender, race, socioeconomic class, professional status, and age detract or add to the power one has. At the same time, there are four factors that impact on this core. One factor is the developmental stage of the supervisor: is he or she a neophyte or experienced? Another factor is the developmental stage of the supervisee: student, extern, intern, new doctorate, or seasoned professional? The third and fourth factors refer to the racial and cultural identity stage of the supervisor and the supervisee.

IMPLICATIONS FOR SUPERVISION

THE SUPERVISOR

Step 1

The first step involves self-examination, which can take place on two levels. On the first level, supervisors from a majority culture can assess their motivations for working with minority students and trainees. This is something that Boyd-Franklin (1989) has advocated for the majority therapist working with minority patients. In those instances where supervisors have no choice in selecting supervisees, they must carefully examine how they feel about the assignment. This type of self-examination can take place in group meetings with other supervisors. Ideally, these supervisors' groups should be facilitated by a majority and a minority supervisor of equal stature in the department or institution.

On the second level, majority supervisors can assess their knowledge base with regard to the value system of the minority supervisee's

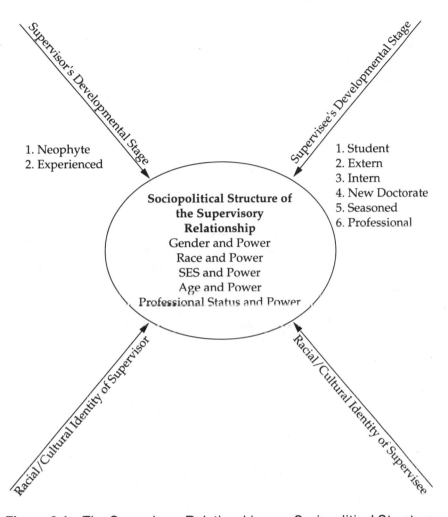

Figure 8.1 The Supervisory Relationship as a Sociopolitical Structure.

culture, with regard to the sociopolitical experience of the supervisee's ethnic group, and with regard to the cultural values of the minority client (particularly the group's attitudes toward psychotherapy and their experiences with the mental health system).

Step 2

This step involves filling in the gaps of knowledge that were uncovered during the self-examination period through didactic learning. The graduate psychology curriculum should provide the necessary courses for students; for practicing psychologists, continuing education programming should meet the need.

Step 3

The following recommendations reflect a compilation of the suggestions in the literature about what to do in the supervision room with the supervisee.

1. A supervisor in a cross-cultural situation should first decide what approach to use. Remington and DaCosta (1989) advocate for a process-oriented approach because by definition it allows for, in fact it insists upon, a discussion of the supervisory relationship. The premise is that conflicts and unconscious motives arising between supervisor and student may be played out in the therapist-client relationship or vice versa (p. 399).
2. The issue of the cultural differences between these two people should be brought up by the supervisor and discussed. This is particularly important in the case of the majority supervisor and minority supervisee. The minority supervisees rarely have peer support groups to discuss this issue.
3. The supervisor can keep in mind the various reactions to the introduction of the topic of cultural differences. In some instances, the supervisee may not have any issues at that point in time. In other instances, the supervisee may have issues but not feel comfortable raising them at the beginning of supervision. And in a third instance, supervisees may have issues they are not aware of. The message must be given to supervisees that it is not only acceptable to raise ethnic, cultural, and racial issues in supervision, but that it is welcomed.
4. Supervisors can make supervisees aware of peer supervision groups or peer discussion groups where these issues can be talked about. The supervisor walks a very fine line and must make sure that supervisees do not get a mixed message that says, I want you to discuss cross-cultural issues, but not here with me; I want you to do it somewhere else. Also, students should not come away with the feeling that their participation in such a peer group will be seen as aggressive or subversive in any way (McNeill et al., 1995).

5. From the very start of supervision, the supervisor should participate in a peer group for supervisors (Remington & DaCosta, 1989; see Table 8.1 for discussion topics). If there is no such group, perhaps a portion of the supervising faculty's staff meeting time should be set aside to discuss supervision. Ideally, the entire process of cross-cultural supervision should be discussed, and supervisors should not wait until there is a problem to call upon colleagues. When discussions occur only around problem issues,

Table 8.1

Topics for Guided Support Group for Supervisors

---

1. Introduction and description of supervisees. Group leaders can take note of demographics such as gender, race, years of experience, graduate program field of study, etc.

2. Establishing a definition of supervision.

3. Delineating the supervisor's responsibilities.

4. Delineating the supervisee's responsibilities.

5. What are some of the common problems that come up in supervision?

6. Have the supervisors ever had a supervisee request another supervisor? If so, did they know the reason?

7. Did they ever get a supervisee transferred to them from another supervisor?

8. Do they think gender impacts on supervision? If so, how?

9. Do they think that cultural and racial differences between supervisor and supervisee influence supervision? If so, how?

10. Do they believe that age differences between the supervisor and supervisee influence supervision? If so, how?

11. What if the supervisee is not just difference but belongs to a group that has been marginalized by society?

12. Are they aware of the institutionalized racism, sexism, and so on that exists in the institutions they are working for?

13. Are they cognizant of the power inherent in the position of supervisor?

---

one runs the risk of blaming the victim and labeling the minority supervisee or all minority supervisees as problems. The discussions should be designed to deal with the supervisor's feelings and not degenerate into student bashing because the supervisor is more comfortable criticizing the student than dealing with his or her own prejudices and anxiety.

6. Supervisors need to make the supervisory triad explicit to the supervisee and discuss possible areas of convergence and divergence in each dyad (supervisor-supervisee, supervisee-client, and supervisor-client; Brown & Landrum-Brown, 1995).

7. When the supervisee has more cultural knowledge about the client than the supervisor, the supervisor needs to demonstrate a willingness to admit the deficiency in knowledge and allow the supervisee to be the teacher in that instance.

The Supervisee

The major implication for the supervisee is the clear need for a forum to discuss ethnic, cultural, and racial issues without the supervisor's being present and without fear of repercussions (McNeill et al., 1995).

Academic Institutions

Academic institutions need to create an environment that is nurturing of the cross-cultural supervisory dyad. To do that there has to be a real commitment to diversity within the department. This commitment can be manifested in a number of ways. One way is to retrain faculty members who are not familiar with and who have not had formal training in cross-cultural competencies. Because the need for cross-cultural training is just recently being recognized and because only recently has a course in cross-cultural issues been made mandatory in some graduate programs, it is very likely that a number of faculty members did not have these courses during their own training. The sheer numbers of faculty who would need this training, the cost of the training, and the degree to which this is seen as a priority are all going to represent barriers to carrying this out.

Another way to demonstrate commitment to diversity is to launch a real search for minority faculty to join the staff. This means making the job attractive. That can include anything from desirable salaries and desirable working areas to not bringing the candidate in on the lowest rung and not piling numerous departmental responsibilities on the faculty member that make it impossible for the new hire to do the research, writing, and publishing that are so often the cornerstone criteria for advancement. The search may require more effort than an ad in the mainstream publications. The people doing the hiring may have to go where the minority faculty are: minority publications, minority state and national organizations, minority conferences, and so on. Additionally, it is important that more than one minority faculty member be hired. Multiple hiring increases the number of supervisors available to do the clinical supervision of testing and psychotherapy on populations the students are not familiar with. Multiple hiring also prevents the lone faculty person from becoming the minority expert or the cultural expert. All too often, an assumption is made that because a faculty person is a member of a minority group, he or she is interested in clinical issues and research related to culture, race, and ethnicity. This often results in the individual's getting assigned all the minority students to advise or supervise or being assigned the department's only cross-cultural course to teach. This person becomes the spokesperson in ethnicity. Multiple hiring decreases the chance of this happening.

Departments can sponsor colloquium series dedicated to cross-cultural issues as another way to increase the exposure of the faculty and students to diversity. There can be workshops for faculty on how to incorporate this area in the courses they already teach (see Chapter 7 regarding the debate over whether or not cross-cultural issues should be one course or incorporated into the entire curriculum). Finally, making cross-cultural courses a part of the core curriculum and developing some measure of cross-cultural competency (such as a comprehensive examination question) will send a message about how this material is valued. The way cross-cultural issues are treated in any graduate department sets the stage for how smoothly the cross-cultural supervisory dyad can exist in that department.

Direct Care Institutions

Cross-cultural supervision does not occur only in graduate schools. In fact, with the limited number of minority faculty and minority students, cross-cultural supervision is probably more likely to occur in direct care settings (hospitals, clinics, Community Mental Health Clinics

[CMHCs], etc.). The ease with which one can conduct cross-cultural supervision may be related to the sensitivity of the agency to diversity. How well can a minority client navigate the agency system? If the client speaks a language other than English, is there a receptionist who can respond to queries in the client's language? How likely is it that the client will encounter a psychotherapist, physician, or nurse of his or her ethnic background? To what extent does the decor of the agency reflect the cultural diversity of the people in the community? Is the client asked to reveal personal material in the presence of unknown housekeeping or office staff because these are the only staff members who can speak the patient's language fluently? The answers to all of these questions have the potential to influence whether and how often cross-cultural issues get raised in supervision.

CHAPTER 9

Cross-Cultural Competencies in Cross-Cultural Training

THE CHALLENGE FACING PSYCHOLOGY

ONE OF THE major challenges facing the field of psychology today is the training of therapists to address the psychological needs of the increasing number of linguistic and culturally diverse families in the United States (Barona, Santos de Barona, Flores, & Gutierrez, 1990; *Population Today*, 1985; Reid, 1986; U.S. Department of Commerce News, 1989). The fact that there continues to be a high dropout rate and a low academic achievement rate for minority children makes this situation even more acute. Because it is virtually impossible to have an equal number of trained specialists who are themselves from the variety of culturally diverse backgrounds as our client population, it is critically important to have the graduates of psychology training programs be knowledgeable about and prepared to address the concerns of this new clientele. Unless this is addressed, therapy will continue to result in outcomes antithetical to the spirit of the mission of the profession. Of course, multicultural training of all psychologists ought not to mitigate the efforts of psychology programs to simultaneously recruit ethnic and culturally different minority students. The goal should really be to train all psychologists to be competent, sensitive, and knowledgeable of the critical factors related to issues of cultural diversity to best serve the culturally different. This knowledge, sensitivity, and awareness ought to be built into the existing psychology training programs.

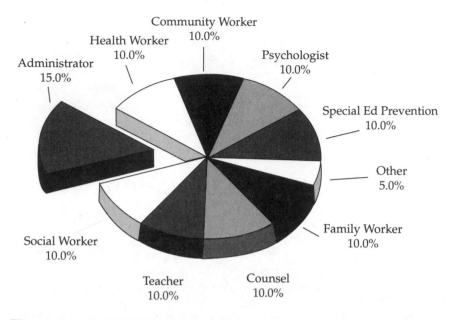

Figure 9.1 A Multi-System Interdisciplinary Model (Discipline Distribution for Successful Acculturator). The impact of culture and language will be examined in each discipline (Gopaul-McNicol, 1997a).

Throughout this book, assessment and counseling skills are suggested for working with ethnic, linguistic, and culturally diverse families. Although those are all strongly recommended, other competencies are needed as prerequisites to best utilize the Multi-CMS model. The primary purpose of this chapter is to propose major competency skills that are needed by all therapists to function as effective helpers. Gopaul-McNicol (1997) highlights some of these competencies for the training of school psychologists (see Figure 9.1).

MAJOR COMPETENCIES NEEDED FOR CROSS-CULTURAL TRAINING

Several researchers (Barona et al., 1990; Carney & Kahn, 1984; Casas et al., 1995; Cummins, 1989; Figueroa et al., 1984; Hills & Strozier, 1992; Kiselica, 1991; McRae & Johnson, 1991; Palmer, Hughes, & Juarez, 1991; Ponterotto & Casas, 1987; Ridley, 1985; Rogers, Close Conoley, Ponterotto, & Wiese, 1992; Sabnani, Ponterotto, & Borodovsky, 1991; Sue,

Arredondo, & McDavis, 1992) have highlighted some of the necessary competencies for psychologists to acquire in working with culturally diverse clients. Table 9.1 summarizes the major multicultural competencies most needed to effectively serve clients from diverse cultural backgrounds.

THERAPIST'S AWARENESS OF OWN CULTURAL BIASES AND VALUES

Arredondo et al. (1996) suggested that all psychologists in training should explore their fundamental significant beliefs and attitudes and

Table 9.1
Cross-Cultural Competencies for Working with Culturally Diverse Families

1. Therapist's Awareness of Own Values and Biases
   - Has knowledge regarding own racial heritage and how it professionally affects the therapeutic process.
   - Has knowledge of how oppression and discrimination personally affect therapists and their work.
2. Cross-Cultural Awareness
   - Has or is acquiring awareness of the variations of different cultural groups with respect to motivational and learning styles, family roles, the impact of migration and relocation.
3. Cross-Cultural Ethical Competence
   - Understands that the treatment of culturally diverse clients by professionals who lack specialized training and expertise is unethical.
4. Cross-Cultural Assessment Competencies
   - Can use assessment instruments appropriately with groups for whom the tests were not standardized.
   - Can articulate the limitations of the instrument with various groups.
5. Cross-Cultural Counseling Competencies
   - Respects the indigenous helping beliefs and practices.
   - Is aware of the institutional impediments that hinder the use of counseling services.
6. Competence in Understanding Interracial Issues
   - Considers issues such as whether the therapist should wait for the client to introduce questions of race.

(continued)

Table 9.1 (Continued)

- Is aware of ways that racial factors may influence the course of treatment.

7. Cross-Cultural Issues in Conflict Resolution
   - Helps the client to identify the ways conflicts affect therapy.

8. Language Competencies
   - Learns to work with bilingual clients either through the use of interpreters or by learning a second language.

9. Competency in the Ability to Work with Interpreters
   - Has knowledge of interpretation procedures; establishes rapport with interpreters.
   - Respects the authority of the interpreter.
   - Knows the kinds of information that tend to get lost during the interpretation procedure.
   - Recognizes the importance of securing accurate translation.

10. Competence in Special Education Prevention
    - Training for special education teachers to function more on preventive specialists than treatment specialists.

11. Competencies in Knowing the Bilingual Education Curriculum
    - Understands what constitutes a bilingual instructional program.

12. Competence in Empowering Families through Community-Based Organizations
    - Assisting families in forming extended family support networks in the community.

13. Competence in Pediatric/Health Psychology
    - Training mental health workers to understand the impact of environmental hazards on a child's ability to learn.

14. Competence in Parent Training
    - Teach parents alternatives to corporal punishment.

15. Cross-Cultural Consultation Competencies
    - Is not averse to seeking consultation with religious healers.
    - Consults with heads of organizations that focus on providing services to individuals of different cultural groups.

16. Cross-Cultural Research Competencies
    - Is familiar with relevant research regarding the mental health of various ethnic and racial groups.
    - Identifies research conducted by respected professionals and viewed as credible by community members.

the impact of those beliefs on the psychological processes and on their ability to respect others different from themselves. They should be allowed to examine their values that impede respect of others' values and beliefs. The adage "Counselor, know thyself" is critical in preventing ethnocentrism, a significant requirement in effective cross-cultural counseling. Culturally competent psychologists ought to be trained to recognize in a teaching or counseling relationship how and when their beliefs, attitudes, and values interfere with providing the best service to their clients. Likewise, training should allow them to recognize the limits of their skills and refer the client to receive more appropriate resources. Training should have at its heart the ability to recognize the sources of discomfort/comfort with respect to differences in culture, ethnicity, and so on, and how these differences are played out in therapy. A culturally competent psychologist is one who tries to avoid making negative judgments about his or her clients even if their worldview differs from that of the counselor's. In other words, they respect and appreciate their clients' differences.

CROSS-CULTURAL AWARENESS

Figueroa, Sandoval, and Merino (1984) emphasized the importance in acquiring awareness of the variations of different cultural groups with respect to motivational and learning styles, expectations related to achievement, exceptionality, and family roles. Medway (1995) emphasized the importance of psychologists' being aware of the impact of migration and relocation. Oftentimes, there are many stresses associated with environmental change—financial, unemployment. It may be necessary for the psychologist to spend some time in the client's ecology to fully appreciate the experiential aspect, so that this cross-cultural knowledge can be applied in psychological assessment, treatment plans, decisions on retention and placement, and so on. Sue and Sue (1990) state that a culturally competent psychologist is one who is actively in the process, becoming aware of his or her own assumptions about human behavior.

CROSS-CULTURAL ETHICAL COMPETENCE

The basis for a specialization in multicultural training for all psychologists grew out of the needs of minorities throughout various systems.

The fundamental premise underlying this position is that the treatment of culturally diverse clients by professionals who lack the specialized training and expertise is unethical, for this is considered delivery of mental health services outside one's area of competence (APA, 1981; Fields, 1979; Korman, 1974; Ridley, 1985). Thus, cross-cultural skill ought to be on a level of parity with other specialized assessment and therapeutic skills. Acceptance of this perspective suggests that a higher and more profound level of training is needed if cross-cultural competence is to be acquired. The key issue is that minority students should not be the sole beneficiary of cross-cultural training. Oftentimes, White professionals, even more than minority professionals, are involved in making critical decisions on the lives of minority clientele. Thus, it is necessary to keep in mind that at the heart of this ethical imperative is the welfare of the client.

CROSS-CULTURAL ASSESSMENT COMPETENCIES

Critical to the assessment of culturally different clients, as discussed in Part 1 of this text, is "the ability to judge the appropriateness of the instrument selected on the basis of linguistic, psychometric, and linguistic criteria" (Figueroa et al., 1984, p. 135). Thus, there must be consideration given to reliability, validity, standards for administration, test interpretation, and test limitations—cognitive as well as socioemotional factors in the assessment procedures. Important to note is when sociocultural factors may be impeding the assessment process. To control for this, it is advised to not limit oneself to formal assessment only. Using only traditional, formal assessment measures is tantamount to misassessment when it pertains to bilingual/multicultural clients. There is a growing body of theoretical and empirical support for a bio-ecological approach to assessment (Armour-Thomas & Gopaul-McNicol, 1997a; Ceci, 1990; Gopaul-McNicol, 1996; Sternberg, 1986), the notion of a dynamically interactive relationship between cognitive processes and cultural experiences nested within contexts that cannot be understood apart from each other. It would appear that although cognitive processes are biologically programmed, how they are developed and expressed depends on the nature and quality of the cultural experiences within the contexts to which individuals are socialized. The exact contributions of biology and culture remain unclear in accounting for intellectual behavior. This line of thinking has led to the conception of intellectual behavior as an inextricable bio-ecological phenomenon and a model of intellectual assessment consistent with this behavior (Chapter 3 examines this bio-ecological approach in detail). In summary, quantitative and qualitative information culled from both forms of assessment would enable a more comprehensive and nondiscriminatory analysis of intellectual functioning of people from culturally and linguistically diverse backgrounds (Armour-Thomas & Gopaul-McNicol, in press, 1997a, 1997b).

Cross-Cultural Counseling Competencies

With respect to cross-cultural training, researchers (McRae & Johnson, 1991; Ponterotto & Casas, 1987; Sue & Zane, 1987) have addressed the need to develop multicultural competencies in awareness, knowledge, expertise, and boundaries of their competence. Psychologists need to be aware of the values, customs, behavioral patterns, religious and indigenous beliefs, and expectancies of families from divergent cultural, linguistic, and ethnic backgrounds. Not only is knowledge necessary about intergroup differences, but about intragroup differences as well. This is critical because within certain groups, there is much diversity. Different familial role structure, different socialization patterns, and different attitudes must be understood to avoid misassessment of a client. Pedersen (1973) developed the triad training method, which is a videotaped, cross-cultural counseling role play that involves three individuals: one person plays the counselor, a second plays the client, and a third plays a pro-counselor (a person from the culture of the client who is a supportive ally to the counselor) or an anticounselor (an antagonistic force from the client's background who promotes understanding of the potential racial or ethnic conflict between the counselor and the client). Both the pro- and anticounselors' roles are important for training; the former aids in the acquisition of knowledge and skills, and the latter was found to be helpful in developing sensitivity and awareness of personal and cultural biases based on different cultural values. Johnson (1982, 1987, 1990) developed a multicultural training program that included the awareness, knowledge, and skill components. This program focuses on experiential exercises that allow trainees to practice and apply the knowledge gained.

COMPETENCE IN UNDERSTANDING INTERRACIAL ISSUES

"Race is an elusive, perplexing, troubling and enduring aspect of life in the United States" (Carter, 1995, p. 1). When a Black person introduces race into psychotherapy, it is often perceived as a form of defense or as an avoidance of a more profound issue. Given the United States' preoccupation with race in the sociopolitical world, it is imperative that students in training are exposed to a psychotherapeutic model that includes race (Carter, 1995). This model includes issues such as whether the therapist should wait for the client to introduce questions of race, how race should be discussed once it has arisen, ways that racial factors may influence the course of treatment, and how one can distinguish between a racial defense and poor psychological functioning. Moreover, knowledge of racial oppression and racial discrimination should be examined in training, so that White therapists can recognize how they benefit from institutionalized and cultural racism. Carter (1995) proposed a race-inclusive model in psychotherapy. All students in training should be exposed to such a model to best understand the influence of race in psychotherapy.

CROSS-CULTURAL ISSUES IN CONFLICT RESOLUTION

The Worldview Congruence Model (Myers, 1991) discusses how interpersonal conflicts are often a result of eight worldview dimensions: psychobehavioral modality, axiology, ontology, ethos, epistemology, logic, concept of time, and concept of self. Brown and Landrum-Brown (1995) illustrated how worldview conflicts affect the client/counselor/supervisor triadic relationship. These conflicts may result in mistrust and resistance. Thus, knowledge of one's view and that of the other parties would prove beneficial in the therapeutic and supervisory relationship. It is necessary for the supervisor to help the counselor and the counselor to help the client to identify the ways these conflicts affect therapy.

LANGUAGE COMPETENCIES

It is necessary for psychologists to be proficient in the language of clients who speak only their native language, but for clients who are more proficient in English, psychologists' bilingual proficiency is not a necessity. Certainly, being competent in oral and written skills facilitates psychologists' ability to establish rapport as well as enables clients to express their feelings more fluidly. Being bilingually proficient also allows the examiner to alternate language as needed and even to be sensitive to dialectical differences. Moreover, being a native speaker of a particular language and being familiar with a client's culture also afford the examiner awareness of subtleties in nonverbal communicative cues. There is no question that being bilingual is preferred, but because it is impossible to learn all of the 120 languages that are commonly found in some metropolitan cities, it is best for all psychologists to be trained in a number of competencies. A psychologist who has been trained in understanding cultural diversity, in working with interpreters, in ecological assessment, and in integrating language proficiency data in report writing can be quite capable of assessing an individual who is from a bilingual home but is more proficient and dominant in English. Thus, this ought not to be ruled out as an option. In addition, culturally skilled psychologists should possess knowledge about the differences in communication styles and how these different styles of communication may clash with that of their clients.

An even greater obstacle in working with linguistically different clients is the impact of dialectical differences on the examinee's performance: "Dialects can pose serious difficulties for the psychologist in understanding the full meaning of clients' responses" (Figueroa et al., 1984, p. 136). Some English-speaking immigrants from Jamaica, for example, speak English Creole, an amalgamation of English, French, Spanish, and African languages. Therefore, although they read and write in English, they speak in a Creole dialect; they may say "him say" but will write "he says." In a testing situation, if examiners are not knowledgeable of the dialectical variants, they may assume a speech deficiency and may misdiagnose the client as speech impaired, a rather common diagnosis given to children who are English-speaking immigrants. A competent psychologist should at least be in the position to ask the question as to whether dialectical factors may be affecting the child's performance. Such children tend to need, not English as a second language (ESL) services, but English as second dialect (ESD; Coelho, 1991; Gopaul-McNicol, 1993). Thus, the focus should be on more opportunities for conversation than on basic interpersonal communication skills involving intensive instruction in vocabulary and grammar characteristic of ESL programs. Children who require ESD services need more opportunity for oral stimulation in the mainstream dialect, where the emphasis is on social appropriateness. In other words, these children simply have to be taught to "discriminate in which situations each dialect will serve them most effectively" (Coelho, 1976, p. 37).

A competent psychologist should be able to apply the information gathered from the clinical interview, family interview, assessment, behavioral observations, and so on. In determining a child's proficiency in a language, if the psychologist taps only the school domain and ignores the home and community, children who have had little or no exposure to school-type vocabulary in their native/second language may appear alingual, that is, possessing little proficiency in either language. In developing an adequate program for language remediation, the psychologist must be knowledgeable of the kinds of conditions that impede or facilitate learning a second language and should aid in creating such an environment for the child. Thus, knowledge of the normal course of language acquisition for monolingual children and bilingual children, issues of motivation, and so on ought to be discussed with the teacher and parent. A well-documented understanding of these issues can be found in Homel, Palif, and Aaronson (1987).

Acquiring Competency in the Ability to Work with Interpreters

In spite of every effort to secure a bilingual psychologist, at times, it is impossible to do so, given the paucity of bilingual psychologists who speak "exotic" languages that are not commonly encountered. Therefore, it is necessary for psychologists to develop competencies in interpretation procedures. Some of these skills can range from establishing rapport with the interpreter, respecting the authority of the interpreter who may be a teacher's aide or paraprofessional or a member of the Parent Teachers Association, knowing the kinds of information that tend to get lost during the interpretation procedure, understanding nonverbal communication cues, and recognizing the importance of securing accurate translation. Also evident should be knowledge of translations that are not as a result of personal evaluation by the interpreter. Moreover, "the psychologist should demonstrate the ability to plan and execute pre-service and in-service programs to prepare interpreters for psychological work with children and to help interpreters follow ethical practices of keeping information confidential" (Figueroa et al., 1984, p. 138). It must be emphasized that, compared to a legal context, testing an individual is a more complex role for the interpreter. In the world of psychology, nonverbal cues can be misinterpreted if the interpreter is not familiar with the client's culture; the psychologist must ensure that kinesthetic cues are not misinterpreted. Figueroa et al. (1984) recommended the use of audio- or videotapes to address this situation, because a precise recording of the testing can be reviewed by the psychologist after completion of the testing.

COMPETENCE IN SPECIAL EDUCATION PREVENTION

During the 1995–1996 academic school year, as we conducted several trainings throughout the State of New York, we were astounded by the sentiments expressed by many practicing psychologists and their supervisors. They repeatedly stated that even if children are not truly handicapped, they have to place them in special education to secure some of the services that these children need. Therefore, they diagnose these "borderline" children as learning disabled when, in fact, the children's profiles are not those of the typical learning-disabled child. An even more disturbing issue that arose is the sentiment that if special education didn't exist, special education teachers would be unemployed; in other words, the institution of special education is necessary not only for the children but for the teachers themselves. There seems to be a maintenance of this system whether it is needed or not. Of course, the fact that children in special education do not receive a high school diploma, thus hindering their chances to go on to college, does not seem to be a major concern for these professionals. To say the least, this is unethical and unprofessional. At this juncture, what is needed is a transitory placement for these borderline children and training for special education teachers to see themselves more as preventive workers than treatment workers. Psychologists can play a significant role in this enterprise. They can serve as consultants to school personnel in assisting special education teachers to utilize their time in working with regular education "at-risk" students to prevent their placement into special education. Thus, a paradigm shift can ensure the continued employment of special education teachers in another capacity (as special education prevention specialists) and, simultaneously, avoid the massive misplacement of children in special education. Training ought to focus on the role of the psychologist in expanding the role of special education teachers to the regular education setting.

COMPETENCIES IN KNOWING THE BILINGUAL EDUCATION CURRICULUM

Knowing what constitutes a bilingual instructional program for bilingual or limited-English-proficient (LEP) children is essential in working with linguistically and culturally diverse children. There is still considerable debate as to whether an ESL or English immersion program is best suited to meet the needs of bilingual children (Homel et al., 1987). Because this debate is expected to continue for years, psychologists ought to be knowledgeable about the available programs and cognizant that some children may benefit from a certain type of program and others may benefit from another. In other words, just as there is no single program for monolingual students, likewise, no single program can fit all bilingual children. It is critical that this be understood by psychologists who serve as consultants to school personnel.

COMPETENCE IN EMPOWERING FAMILIES THROUGH COMMUNITY-BASED ORGANIZATIONS

Competent psychologists have to be able to direct their families to the community-based organizations that can support the school by utilizing their resources in working with handicapped children. Afterschool tutorial programs, day care centers, free lunch programs, and free clinic care are some examples of community supports that can be used to supplement the needed services that the schools are unable to provide. Utilizing places of worship, social service agencies, and other outside systems are ways of empowering families. For example, there are afterschool transportation services that can transfer children to and from therapy sessions. Tapping these community resources "is sometimes the single most important interaction in facilitating the possibility of treatment" (Boyd-Franklin, 1989, p. 156). In addition, if certain necessary services are not available in a particular community, assisting families in forming extended family support networks should be part of the responsibility of the school psychologist.

COMPETENCE IN PEDIATRIC/HEALTH PSYCHOLOGY

Given the increase in the reported cases of asthma and lead poisoning in urban settings, in particular in some of the New York City school districts such as the Bronx and Brooklyn (Brody, 1996), it is critical that psychologists begin to explore the impact of these factors on a child's ability to learn and pay attention. Brody (1996) presents the findings of Dr. Herbert Needleman of the University of Pittsburgh, who found that high levels of lead in the bones of an individual are most likely to lead to attention difficulties, intellectual deficits, aggression, and other social problems.

The New York State Department of Education has already established a Healthy School Project in several suburban school districts. Con Edison has been part of this initiative by linking its health awareness program to this project. All of these efforts are aimed at assisting families in detecting early in their child's education any medical problems that may impede their child's ability to learn or function effectively in the school system. This is essential in the accurate assessment of a child's handicapping condition. Ruling out any medical problems is one way of preventing misdiagnosis and misplacement.

COMPETENCIES IN PARENT TRAINING

Mental health workers can play a major role in educating immigrant parents about the educational and social differences in the U.S. systems (Gopaul-McNicol, Thomas, & Irish, 1991). They can encourage them to attend PTA meetings, explain the issues of confidentiality regarding school records, help them establish contact with community resources, and all in all, assist in the acculturation process. All mental health workers can teach parents alternatives to corporal punishment. Mental health workers also need to alert parents to the reality of special education and the need for them to question the motives of the teacher. Generally speaking, immigrant parents trust their children's teachers and allow placement in special education if the teacher recommends it. They need to be taught about the special education system, as this is a foreign concept to most of them. Thomas and Gopaul-McNicol (1991) discuss this in detail.

Helping parents to understand the social and emotional adjustment difficulties their children are experiencing is of major importance in parent training. In general, assisting in the acculturation process involves nine important points:

1. Education about the differences in the U.S. education and social systems, with emphasis on alternative disciplinary strategies, the meaning of educational neglect, and the importance of attending parent teacher meetings.
2. Family empowerment, with emphasis on their legal rights.
3. Understanding the family role changes and their effect on acculturation (see Chapter 7).
4. Improving communication between parents and children.
5. Teaching parents how to build or maintain positive self-esteem in their children.
6. Coping with racism.
7. Teaching parents what support their children need at home and the importance of prioritizing their time.
8. Teaching parents how to cope with rejection from their children when the children are embarrassed by their parents' accent.
9. Teaching immigrants how to endorse the concept of biculturalism, so that they do not have to live between two worlds.

The question most often asked by parents is "How can I raise children without disciplining them? I only know the way I was raised at home." The answer involves not only teaching parents the principles of assertive discipline but helping parents to recognize that because their children are the first generation of Americans, many of the parents' traditional cultural values will not be passed on to them. Expediting the process of "Americanization" in a radical way may leave the parents feeling stripped of cultural pride. It is necessary for parents to understand there are laws governing, for instance, child abuse, but they must also understand that acculturation for first-generation immigrants is a different process from acculturation for second- and third-generation immigrants. Although some of the traditional values will be passed on, inevitably their children will not have the tremendous allegiance to their native countries that the parents do. Parents must understand that strong cultural identity may dissipate over time, as each new generation becomes more Americanized. However, immigrant parents ought not to be expected to abandon all of their values, because this can create much anxiety and despair, leaving them vulnerable and immobilized in a sometimes hostile environment. Instead, these parents need to be taught that the essence and beauty of their culture are retained in some of their traditional values and, to some extent, some of these values can be beneficial in helping children to cope. What immigrant families need to be taught is how to take the best from both cultures as they attempt to assimilate in their new country.

CROSS-CULTURAL COMPETENCIES AT THE UNIVERSITY LEVEL

In addition to those competencies listed in Table 9.1 and in addition to the issues raised in Chapters 7 and 8, faculty members in psychology programs need to acquire competencies in the areas listed below: consultation and supervision, research, and teaching.

CROSS-CULTURAL CONSULTATION AND SUPERVISION

Cross-cultural factors that affect consultation and supervision include interracial therapist-client differences, language or dialectical (verbal/nonverbal) differences, social and/or occupational/economic status differences, and differences due to cultural isolation (Brown & Landrum-Brown, 1995). Lefley (1986) emphasized that ongoing evaluation of a counselor's multicultural development also needs to be a focus in cross-cultural training. Likewise, educational differences among the client, counselor, and supervisor, and differences in immigration status and geographic origin can affect the perspectives of supervision. This is because any of the above differences can affect the supervisory relationship with respect to content, process, and outcome. Relatedly, these differences can result in resistance to corrective feedback because of cultural misunderstandings. This can affect the supervisory relationship to the extent that some supervisees systematically refuse to respond to the suggestions of their supervisors to maintain the cultural relevance of their therapeutic approaches.

Brown and Landrum-Brown (1995) outlined and critiqued several supervision theories that consider the relevant cross-cultural dimensions that are likely to influence the supervisory process. What is still desperately needed is an expansion of these supervisory models to embody the intercultural dynamic interaction.

Family consultation is in dire need of examination because the concept of family has changed immensely over the past 15 years. The nuclear family model, with two parents and two children, is no longer the norm; many cultures emphasize the extended family as a strong financial and emotional support system (Halsell Miranda, 1993) to address the growing change in the family structure.

CROSS-CULTURAL RESEARCH

In addition to the ethical guidelines suggested for all mental health workers, the American Psychological Association (1993), Pedersen (1995), Ponterotto and Casas (1991), Tapp, Kelman, Triandis, Wrightsman, and Coelho (1974), and Wrenn (1985) outlined ethical considerations in conducting cross-cultural research:

1. It is necessary to understand the prevailing psychosocial problems, identify the psychocultural strengths, and examine the community involvement in each culture.
2. It is important to avoid the dangers of defining everyone's reality according to particular cultural assumptions; in other words, it is important to understand the client's/culture's worldview.
3. It is important to consult colleagues in and out of the culture to help make good ethical judgments.
4. It is critical to attend to the technical problems of equivalent measurement across cultures; failure to do so may result in inaccurate interpretations and potentially damaging consequences to the culture being studied.
5. It is important to avoid overuse of a particular culture or a particular population.
6. It is noteworthy that the definition of *privacy* varies culturally; therefore, what may be routine to a Westerner may be highly intrusive to the host culture. Behaviors that are private to a culture may

not be intended for open and public discussion by noncommunity members.

7. Research should be beneficial not only to the researcher, but to the host community as well: the population studied should be enhanced by the research.

CROSS-CULTURAL TEACHING: A PROPOSED
MULTICULTURAL CURRICULUM

Bernal and Padilla (1982) called for a multicultural training philosophy. The competencies described above should be infused into the existing psychology program, with each student receiving a one-year internship in a multiethnic/multicultural/multilinguistic school district. In addition, the curriculum should have an interdisciplinary approach, utilizing the contributions from related fields such as social work, psychiatry, and anthropology. Intradisciplinary work, by way of exposure to cross-cultural issues in clinical, counseling, social, developmental, and educational psychology, can be quite beneficial in cross-cultural training. Moreover, areas such as psycholinguistics, bilingual/multicultural education, cross-cultural theory, and cross-cultural counseling are all requisites in developing cross-cultural competence. Ethical and legal issues in multicultural assessment, treatment, consultation, supervision, research, and so on should be infused in each course, not offered only as a separate course. Ridley (1985) suggested that every effort should be made to ferret out principles that are universal in nature, so that a basis for determining where cultural variability begins and cultural generalization ends can be established. Exposure to various cultural groups should afford students the opportunity to be part of a viable programmatic experience.

Rogers et al. (1992) found that 60% of the doctoral and nondoctoral programs they surveyed offered only one course devoted specifically to multicultural issues; 63% of those programs surveyed offered two to five courses. Seventy-five percent of the programs made at least one multicultural course a requirement. Rogers et al. (1992) also found that 27% of the programs they surveyed spent less than 5% of their time on courses related to minority issues; 40% did not spend any time at all on courses addressing a multicultural content, and most of the programs

(94%) did not require exposure to a foreign language course. Thus, the need to develop a specific multicultural curriculum is crucial.

Implementation of the Curriculum

To accomplish this innovative multicultural training program, a step-by-step guideline is outlined below.

1. A written academic policy must emphasize a clear statement of purpose and commitment to cultural diversity, as well as the consequences to the program if these policies are violated. Included in this statement must be definite, quantifiable program objectives that must be achieved in a particular time frame.
2. Inclusion of cultural and ethnic content should be infused in each course, not taught as a single course only. Thus, psychological assessment should be taught first to expose students to adherence of standardized procedures, and then students should be taught how to step away from standardized testing. Likewise, treatment should allow for cultural consideration throughout the therapeutic courses.
3. There should be a more aggressive recruitment of faculty members and students of various cultural backgrounds. Working with an ethnically diverse student and faculty body adds enrichment to the program, encouraging one to view issues from various perspectives.
4. Faculty members should be encouraged to update their cross-cultural expertise by attending continuing education courses, seminars, and so on. The university should make a reduction in their teaching load for one year to allow for this cross-cultural training.
5. A consultant or a full-time faculty member with cross-cultural expertise should be available to consult with all faculty members to assist them in redesigning the curricula to reflect diverse cultural content.
6. Funds should be set aside for a few research students to be assigned strictly for this cross-cultural thrust: building a cross-cultural resource file, assisting in student and faculty recruitment, linking with community people to recruit more ethnic

minority practicum supervisors, coordinating experts of different cultural backgrounds to speak at colloquiums, and so on.

7. A faculty member and several students should be designated to
represent ethnic students' concerns.

8. Linkages should be formed with other departments within the
university to identify existing cross-cultural courses and experts
in cross-cultural studies.

9. Faculty members should be encouraged to attend international
conferences, not only in European countries, but in "third-world"
countries as well.

10. For the first two years, an ongoing review of the program to ensure that the goals are being met should be done on a monthly
basis at regular staff meetings. After two years of smooth functioning, review should be done on a quarterly basis, and after five
years, an annual basis should suffice. Every faculty member
should be required to sit in on these meetings.

11. Without all of the above in place and without financial support to
fund all of these innovative efforts, failure is most likely to occur.
Because the ultimate goal of innovation should be institutional-
ization, many financial endowments are needed (Ridley, 1985).

Johnson (1982, 1987, 1990) developed a two-part course that included
theory, current research, and a laboratory experiential-type section.
Practica in all areas of training should be available to ensure that all
students receive hands-on training in working with culturally and linguistically different clients. Rogers et al. (1992) found that 69% of pro
gram directors estimated that students were exposed to minority
clients less than 25% of their time during their practicum and internship experiences. Of even more concern, they found that almost one-
third of the programs surveyed reported that students spent 0–5% of
their experiential training time with minority clients. This suggests
that a large percentage of "school psychology students have limited or
no direct exposure to culturally diverse clients during field training"
(p. 607). Mio (1989), in his multicultural counseling course, encouraged
students to interact with a person from a different culture on a regular
basis over the course of the semester. It was found that those students
who were matched with an immigrant were rated as more sensitive

than students who did not regularly interact with a culturally different person at the end of the semester. Clearly, the experiential component helps promote cultural awareness and knowledge of another culture.

A multicultural curriculum should be multifaceted, consisting of a combination of assessment, review of the ethnic literature, personal involvement, and the development of a small classroom group project (Parker, Valley, & Geary, 1986). This approach utilizes the cognitive, affective, and behavioral domains. Students should first be assessed on their knowledge, attitudes, and perceptions of cross-cultural experiences, as well as their comfort level in interacting with others from different ethnic and racial groups. This assessment process serves as a guide to the professor for future training. Part Two of the course involves readings and discussions about racial and ethnic literature. Part Three is action-oriented in that it involves behavioral activities geared to helping students increase cultural knowledge, sensitivity, and effectiveness. Students initially observe from a distance via videotapes and so on and gradually begin to participate directly. In the final stage, the students are expected to work on a small group activity in class. Such a project allows students to become aware of their own stereotypical values about other racial and ethnic groups.

Multicultural training should also focus on the influence of race in racial identity development (Carter, 1995), with recommendations for White professors who teach multicultural students and cross-cultural issues, as well as minority professors who teach cross-cultural issues to a White student population.

In conclusion, to prevent the marginalization of the psychology profession, there is a dire need to seriously address the change in population demographics, particularly in the metropolitan areas. A true commitment to multicultural training requires at minimum the implementation of all of the above. If a multicultural program has only the bare skeleton of a commitment, it creates no more than false generosity (Freire, 1970), dishonesty, and continued disrespect. The goal should be to produce competent psychologists capable of working with clients from any linguistic, cultural, or ethnic background.

CHAPTER 10

Implications for Future
Research and Clinical Work

THROUGHOUT THIS book, the authors have discussed a number of strategies in the areas of assessment, treatment, teaching, training, and supervision to improve the functioning of culturally diverse families. This chapter briefly recapitulates the approaches endorsed in light of their implications for culturally diverse families, mental health professionals, and researchers. The research has delineated pedagogical, assessment, and intervention strategies that provide a guide for the development of future educational policies that in turn lay a foundation for clinical practices.

The responsibility to adequately train mental health professionals falls upon the shoulders of organizations such as the American Psychological Association. At this time researchers have identified a number of factors that operate together in such a way that such a training program can take place (Cummins, 1984); consequently, policymakers can create and fund programs that would prevent the maladjustment of culturally diverse families.

The four-tier bio-ecological assessment system (Armour-Thomas & Gopaul-McNicol, 1997a) was developed in response to the authors' concern that standardized tests of intelligence provided an incomplete appraisal of children's cognitive functioning. Guided by the assumptions of the authors' emerging bio-ecological model, a number of cognitive enhancement procedures were used in conjunction with the traditional IQ measure, the WISC-III, to identify cognitive strengths and weaknesses of children. We are encouraged with the results that demonstrate that improvement on intellectual tasks are to be expected when children are (a) allowed opportunity to contextualize words in sentences; (b) given time and paper and pencil to solve verbal problems involving memory and quantitative reasoning; and (c) given time and opportunity to understand and solve spatial problems involving memory, understanding, and reasoning.

Perhaps as important, intervention studies should be longitudinal in design to allow sufficient time for reinforcement and generalizability of effects to other contexts. It may well be that Head Start and other intervention programs for improving intelligence showed few enduring results due to the brevity of the treatment. During the course of development of some children, threatening person-environment interactions may far outweigh the sustaining ones. To offset the negative impact of the former, longer and more enriching interventions are likely to produce more lasting cognitive change.

In general, all of the models and issues raised in Parts Two and Three of this book should be considered for further research and clinical work. The use of the Multi-CMS model for treatment should be examined in more detail in research studies. Likewise, the impact of second language or dialects such as Creole and ebonics should be explored in light of new findings that second language acquisition dramatically affects learning. The suggestions proposed in Chapter 6 for teachers who work with linguistic and culturally diverse children should be implemented in a research program for the next decade. We may witness an improvement in performance with this population, if teachers themselves hone their cross-cultural clinical and educational skills.

Several issues and questions that have been raised throughout the course of this book need further investigation:

1. Research that examines the interaction of all three stems of the supervisory triad.
2. Research on the Black-White supervisory dyad that takes into account level of racial identity of both supervisor and supervisee and looks at how this impacts on satisfaction with supervision.

3. Research on the impact of peer supervision groups designed to provide a forum for discussion of problems with supervisors: Do they really help?

4. Research that recognizes the complexity of the supervisory dyad in which the race of the supervisor and supervisee are the same, but the individuals are from different cultures.

5. The development of rating scales for supervisors and supervisees to assess the quality of their experiences.

6. The use of those scales to compare what happens in different supervision triangles.

7. Research on how universities can train mental health workers in a more interdisciplinary fashion to enhance their ability to provide psychological services.

8. Collection of normative data on diverse cultural groups regarding parenting practices.

9. Development of methods for assessing parenting skills that are not so heavily dependent on verbal skills.

10. Examination of the impact on parenting skills of parent-child separation due to immigration.

11. Studies determining to what extent, if any, acculturation strains parent-child relationships.

12. Examination of the impact of acculturation on discipline practices.

13. Studies that look at the impact of socioeconomic status on parenting style.

14. Research into whether therapists make differential judgments about parenting skills based on culture, ethnicity, race, or religion.

15. Development of parenting scales that reflect issues germane to a wide variety of cultures.

16. Studies devoted to the development of ethnic identity in children.

17. Research into whether parents of one ethnicity can transmit culture and enhance ethnic identity to children of another ethnicity (i.e., in cross-racial/ethnic adoption).

18. Studies determining whether the definition of age-appropriate behaviors differs from culture to culture.

19. Studies determining whether the definition of gender-appropriate behaviors differs from culture to culture.

20. Studies determining whether the children of mixed marriages develop an ethnic identity at the same rate as children of endogamous marriages.
21. Evaluation of parent training programs for their effectiveness across cultures.

The challenges set forth in this book in working with culturally diverse families leave the interested researcher with a research agenda for the next decade.

APPENDIX

A Comprehensive Instrument to Assess Cross-Cultural Competencies

ENTAL HEALTH professionals can assess their own levels of cross-cultural competency by using the instrument found in this Appendix. This instrument was based on the works of experts, a review of empirical data, and an examination of several existing competency instruments: D'Andrea, Daniels, and Heck (1991); Gopaul-McNicol (1997); Ponterotto, Rieger, Barrett, and Sparks (1994); Rogers and Lopez's Delphi Poll, currently being conducted; Grantham's (1996) final report of the Cultural Competence Workgroup; and the National Council of School Psychologists, which recommended professional core competency areas for practicing school psychologists.

Instructions: The following cross-cultural competency instrument (Gopaul-McNicol, 1997) is designed to provide students/trainers with information to determine their effectiveness as cross-cultural mental health workers. It is not a test, and no grade will be given. Please rate the competencies using the 3-point Likert scale provided at the side of each item. Feel free to elaborate as necessary.

THEORETICAL PERSPECTIVES

Cross-culturally skilled psychologists should have knowledge about:

1. Different or deficit theories.	1 Important	2 Not Applicable	3 Unimportant
2. The degree to which the major theoretical paradigms in psychology emphasize a Eurocentric ideology.	1 Important	2 Not Applicable	3 Unimportant

THERAPIST'S OWN VALUES

Cross-culturally skilled psychologists should have knowledge about:

1. Own worldview, assumptions, values, beliefs, and priorities, and own cultural heritage.	1 Important	2 Not Applicable	3 Unimportant
2. How their own cultural background and experiences, attitudes, values, and biases influence delivery of psychological services.	1 Important	2 Not Applicable	3 Unimportant
3. Limits of their own competencies, including the limits of their own language competencies if working with bilingual clients.	1 Important	2 Not Applicable	3 Unimportant

CROSS-CULTURAL AWARENESS

Cross-culturally skilled psychologists should have knowledge about:

1. The specific cultural groups that they work with.	1 Important	2 Not Applicable	3 Unimportant

2. The cultural context, belief system, heritage, the history of oppression of the client.	1 Important	2 Not Applicable	3 Unimportant

CROSS-CULTURAL ETHICS

Cross-culturally skilled psychologists should have knowledge about:

1. Ethical issues when working with interpreters (e.g., confidentiality).	1 Important	2 Not Applicable	3 Unimportant
2. Laws and regulations that apply to culturally diverse families.	1 Important	2 Not Applicable	3 Unimportant

ASSESSMENT

Cross-culturally skilled psychologists should have knowledge about:

1. Sources of test bias.	1 Important	2 Not Applicable	3 Unimportant
2. Nonbiased assessment and the process of adapting available instruments to assess culturally diverse families.	1 Important	2 Not Applicable	3 Unimportant
3. Judging the appropriateness of instruments selected on the basis of linguistic, psychometric, and cultural criteria.	1 Important	2 Not Applicable	3 Unimportant
4. Adapting measures created for nonminority children for use with culturally diverse families.	1 Important	2 Not Applicable	3 Unimportant

REPORT WRITING

Cross-culturally skilled psychologists should have knowledge about:

	1	2	3
1. The importance of integrating cultural background information and language background of the family and child.	Important	Not Applicable	Unimportant
2. Reporting deviations from standardization during administration of standardized tests.	Important	Not Applicable	Unimportant

COUNSELING

Cross-culturally skilled psychologists should have knowledge about:

	1	2	3
1. The importance of perceiving the problem within the client's cultural and social context.	Important	Not Applicable	Unimportant
2. Incorporating knowledge about the stresses of being a minority into the counseling approach.	Important	Not Applicable	Unimportant
3. Designing and delivering culturally appropriate prevention and counseling strategies.	Important	Not Applicable	Unimportant

RACE ISSUES

Cross-culturally skilled psychologists should have knowledge about:

	1	2	3
The interrelationship between the client's racial identity development and the effect on the client's coping behaviors.	Important	Not Applicable	Unimportant

LANGUAGE

Cross-culturally skilled psychologists should have knowledge about:

The influence of second language acquisition on children's performances.	1 Important	2 Not Applicable	3 Unimportant

WORKING WITH INTERPRETERS

Cross-culturally skilled psychologists should have knowledge about:

1. The problems involved in translating test items from one language to another.

   1 Important   2 Not Applicable   3 Unimportant

2. The effects of translation on validity, reliability, and test interpretation during assessment.

   1 Important   2 Not Applicable   3 Unimportant

3. The competencies needed by interpreters, translation techniques, professional conduct, relevant knowledge.

   1 Important   2 Not Applicable   3 Unimportant

CONSULTATION

Cross-culturally skilled psychologists should have knowledge about:

1. Actively learning about other cultures through inservice training, continuing education, working with individuals from other cultures.

   1 Important   2 Not Applicable   3 Unimportant

2. Seeking consultation and supervision from other professionals skilled in delivering services to culturally diverse clients.

   1 Important   2 Not Applicable   3 Unimportant

3. Consultation theory and how it can be applied to culturally diverse populations.

   1 Important   2 Not Applicable   3 Unimportant

RESEARCH

Cross-culturally skilled psychologists should have knowledge about:

1. The ethical implications of conducting research with culturally diverse populations.

1	2	3
Important	Not Applicable	Unimportant

2. Creating research projects that are ethnically valid.

1	2	3
Important	Not Applicable	Unimportant

References

Allen, B. A., & Boykin, A. W. (1992). Children and the educational process: Alienating cultural discontinuity through prescriptive pedagogy. *School Psychology Review, 21*(4), 586–596.

American Psychiatric Association. (1987). *Diagnostic and statistical manual of mental disorders* (3rd ed. rev.). Washington, DC: Author.

American Psychiatric Association. (1994). *Diagnostic and statistical manual of mental disorders* (4th ed.). Washington, DC: Author.

American Psychological Association. (1993). Guidelines for providers of psychological services to ethnic, linguistic and culturally diverse populations. *American Psychologist, 48,* 45–48.

Aponte, H. (1976). The family-school interview: An ecostructural approach. *Family Process, 15*(3), 303–311.

Aponte, H., & Van Deusen, J. (1981). Structural family therapy. In A. Gurman & D. Kniskern (Eds.), *Handbook of family therapy* (pp. 27–37). New York: Brunner/Mazer.

Armour-Thomas, E. (1992). Intellectual assessment of children from culturally diverse backgrounds. *School Psychology Review, 21*(4), 552–565.

Armour-Thomas, E., & Gopaul-McNicol, S. (1997a). Examining the correlates of learning disability: A bio-ecological approach. *Journal of Social Distress and the Homeless, 6*(2), 140–165.

Armour-Thomas, E., & Gopaul-McNicol, S. (1997b). A bio-ecological approach to intellectual assessment. *Cultural Diversity and Mental Health, 3*(2), 25–39.

Armour-Thomas, E., & Gopaul-McNicol, S. (in press). *Assessing intelligence: A bio-cultural model.* Thousand Oaks, CA: Sage.

Arredondo-Down, P. (1981). Personal loss and grief as a result of migration. *Personnel and Guidance Journal, 58,* 376–378.

Asby, D. (1975). Empathy: Let's get the hell on with it. *Counseling Psychologist, 5*(2), 10–15.

Auerswald, E. (1968). Interdisciplinary versus ecological approach. *Family Process, 7,* 204.

Axelson, J. A. (1993). *Counseling and development in a multicultural society* (2nd ed.). Belmont, CA: Brooks/Cole.

Bandura, A. (1969). *Principles of behavior modification.* New York: Holt.

Baptiste, D. A. (1984). Marital and family therapy with racially/culturally intermarried stepfamilies: Issues and guidelines. *Family Relations, 33,* 373–380.

Baron, J. (1981). Reflective thinking as a goal of education. *Intelligence, 5,* 291–309.

Baron, J. (1982). Personality and intelligence. In R. J. Sternberg (Ed.), *Handbook of human intelligence.* New York: Cambridge University Press.

Barona, A., Santos de Barona, A., Flores, A. A., & Gutierrez, M. H. (1990). Critical issues in training school psychologists to serve minority school children. In A. Barona & E. Garcia (Eds.), *Children at risk: Poverty, minority status and other issues in educational equity* (pp. 187–200). Washington, DC: National Association of School Psychologists.

Bem, S. L. (1974). The measurement of psychological androgyny. *Journal of Counseling and Clinical Psychology, 42,* 155–162.

Bernal, M. E., & Padilla, A. M. (1982). Status of minority curricula and training in clinical psychology. *American Psychologist, 37,* 780–787.

Bernal, M. J., & Castro, F. G. (1994). Are clinical psychologists prepared for service and research with ethnic minorities? *American Psychologist, 49*(9), 797–805.

Bernal, M. J., & Knight, G. M. (Eds.). (1993). *Ethnic identity: Formation and transmission among Hispanics and other minorities.* Albany: State University of New York Press.

Berry, J. W., Kim, U., Minde, T., & Mok, D. (1987). Comparative studies of acculturative stress. *International Migration Review, 21*(3), 491–511.

Binet, A., & Simon, T. (1905). Méthodes nouvelles pour le diagnostic du niveau intellectual des anormaux. *L'Annee psychologique, 11,* 245–336.

Bowen, M. (1978). *Family therapy in clinical practice.* New York: Jason Aronson.

Boyd-Franklin, N. (1989). *Black families in therapy.* New York: Guilford Press.

Boyd-Franklin, N., & Garcia-Preto, N. (1994). Family therapy: A closer look at African American and Hispanic women. In L. Comas-Diaz & B. Greene (Eds.), *Women of color: Integrating ethnic and gender identities in psychotherapy* (pp. 239–264). New York: Guilford Press.

Boykin, A. W. (1983). The academic performance of Afro-American children. In J. T. Spence (Ed.), *Achievement and achievement motives* (pp. 322–371). San Francisco: Freeman.

Brand, C. R., & Deary, I. J. (1982). *Intelligence and "inspection time": A model for intelligence.* Berlin: Springer-Verlag.

Brice, J. (1982). West Indian families. In M. McGoldrick, J. K. Pearce, & J. Giordana (Eds.), *Ethnicity and family therapy* (pp. 123–133). New York: Guilford Press.

Brice-Baker, J. (1996). Jamaican families. In M. McGoldrick, J. Pearce, & J. Giordano (Eds.), *Ethnicity and family therapy* (2nd ed.). New York: Guilford Press.

Brody, J. (1996). Aggressiveness and delinquency in boys is linked to lead in bones. *New York Times, Health Section K*, p. 4.

Bronfenbrenner, V. (1977). Towards an experimental ecology of human development. *American Psychologist, 45*, 513–530.

Brown, M. T., & Landrum-Brown, J. (1995). Counselor supervision: Cross-cultural perspectives. In J. G. Ponterotto, J. M. Casas, L. A. Suzuki, & C. M. Alexander (Eds.), *Handbook of multicultural counseling* (pp. 263–286). Thousand Oaks, CA: Sage.

Burnam, M. A., Hough, R. L., Kamo, M., Escobar, J. I., & Telles, C. A. (1987). Acculturation and lifetime prevalence of psychiatric disorders among Mexican Americans in Los Angeles. *Journal of Health and Social Behavior, 28*, 89–102.

Canino, I. A., & Spurlock, J. (1994). *Culturally diverse children and adolescents: Assessment, diagnosis and treatment.* New York: Guilford Press.

Carlson, J. S. (1985). The issue of g: Some relevant questions. *Behavioral and Brain Sciences, 8*(2), 224–225.

Carney, C. G., & Kahn, K. B. (1984). Building competencies for effective cross-cultural counseling: A developmental view. *The Counseling Psychologist, 12*(1), 111–119.

Carr, T. H., & McDonald, J. L. (1985). Different approach to individual differences. *Behavioral and Brain Sciences, 8*(2), 225–227.

Carraher, T. N., Carraher, D., & Schliemann, A. D. (1985). Mathematics in the streets and in schools. *British Journal of Development Psychology, 3*, 21–29.

Carroll, J. B. (1993). *Human cognitive abilities.* Cambridge, England: Cambridge University Press.

Carter, R. (1995). *The influence of race and racial identity in psychotherapy.* New York: Wiley.

Cayleff, S. (1986). Ethical issues in counseling gender, race and culturally distinct groups. *Journal of Counseling and Development, 54*, 345–347.

Ceci, S. (1990). *On intelligence: More or less.* Englewood Cliffs, NJ: Prentice-Hall.

Coelho, E. (1976). West Indian students in the secondary schools. *Tesl Talk, 7*(4), 37–46.

Coelho, E. (1991). *Caribbean students in Canadian schools.* Ontario, Canada: Pippin.

Cohen, R. (1969). Conceptual styles, culture conflict, and non-verbal tests of intelligence. *American Anthropologist, 71*(5), 828–857.

Comas-Diaz, L., & Greene, B. (Eds.). (1994). *Women of color: Integrating ethnic and gender identities in psychotherapy.* New York: Guilford Press.

Comas-Diaz, L., & Griffith, E. (Eds.). (1988). *Clinical guidelines in cross-cultural mental health.* New York: Wiley.

Cook, D. (1994). Racial identity in supervision. *Counselor Education and Supervision, 34*(2), 132–141.

Copeland, E. J. (1982). Minority populations and traditional counseling programs: Some alternatives. *Counselor Education and Supervision, 21,* 187–193.

Cummins, J. (1984). *Bilingualism and special education: Issues in assessment and pedagogy.* San Diego, CA: College Hill Press.

Cummins, J. (1989). A theoretical framework for bilingual special education. *Exceptional Children, 56*(2), 111–119.

Dana, R. H. (1993). *Multicultural assessment perspectives for professional psychology.* Boston: Allyn & Bacon.

D'Andrea, M., Daniels, J., & Heck, R. (1991). The multicultural awareness-knowledge-skills survey (MAKSS). *Journal of Counseling and Development, 70,* 149–150.

Davidson, J. (1992). Theories about black-white interracial marriage: A clinical perspective. *Journal of Multicultural Counseling and Development, 20,* 150–157.

Davis, L. E., & Proctor, E. K. (1989). *Race, gender and class: Guidelines for practice with individuals, families and groups.* Englewood Cliffs, NJ: Prentice-Hall.

De Avila, E. (1974, November–December). The testing of minority children: A neo-Piagetian approach. *Today's Education,* 72–75.

deHirsch, K., Jansky, J., & Langford, S. W. (1986). *Predicting reading failure.* New York: Harper & Row.

Dillard, J. M. (1983). *Multicultural counseling.* Chicago: Nelson-Hall.

Domokos-Cheng Ham, M. A. (1989a). Empathetic understanding: A skill for joining with immigrant families. *Journal of Strategic and Systemic Therapies, 8*(2), 36–40.

Domokos-Cheng Ham, M. A. (1989b). Family therapy with immigrant families: Constructuring a bridge between different world views. *Journal of Strategic and Systemic Therapies, 8,* 1–13.

Draguns, J. G. (1987). Psychological disorders across cultures. In P. Pedersen (Ed.), *Handbook of cross-cultural counseling and therapy* (pp. 55–62). New York: Praeger.

Ellis, A. (1974). *Humanistic psychotherapy: The rational emotive approach.* New York: McGraw-Hill.

Espin, O. (1994). Feminist approaches. In L. Comas-Diaz & B. Greene (Eds.), *Women of color: Integrating ethnic and gender identities in psychotherapy* (pp. 265–286). New York: Guilford Press.

Esquivel, G. (1985). Best practices in the assessment of limited English proficient and bilingual children. In A. Thomas & J. Grimes (Eds.), *Best practices in school psychology* (Vol. 1, pp. 113–123). Washington, DC: National Association of School Psychologists.

Evans-Pritchard, E. (1962). *Social anthropology and other essays.* New York: Free Press.

Eysenck, H. J. (1982). Introduction. In H. J. Eysenck (Ed.), *A model for intelligence.* Berlin: Springer Verlag.

Falicov, C. (1988). Learning to think culturally in family therapy training. In H. Little, D. Breunlin, & D. Schwartz (Eds.), *Handbook of family therapy training and supervision* (pp. 335–357). New York: Guilford Press.

Farber, B. (1973). *Family and kinship in modern society.* Glenview, IL: Scott Foresman.

Feurstein, R. (1979). *The dynamic assessment of retarded performers.* Baltimore: University Park Press.

Fields, S. (1979). Mental health and the melting pot. *Innovations, 6*(2), 2–3.

Figueroa, A. F., Sandoval, J., & Merino, B. (1984). School psychology and limited English proficient children: New competencies. *Journal of School Psychology, 22,* 133–143.

Freire, P. (1970). *Pedagogy of the oppressed.* New York: Seabury Press.

Frisby, C. L. (1992). Issues and problems in the influence of culture on the psychoeducational needs of African American children. *School Psychology Review, 21*(4), 532–551.

Gardner, H. (1993). *Multiple intelligences.* New York: Basic Books.

Gladstein, G. (1983). Understanding empathy: Integrating counseling, developmental and social psychology perspective. *Journal of Counseling Psychology, 30*(4), 467–482.

Goodstein, C. (1990). America's cities: The new immigrants in the schools. *Crisis, 98*(5), 17–29.

Gopaul-McNicol, S. (1993). *Working with West Indian families.* New York: Guilford Press.

Gopaul-McNicol, S. (1997a). *Multicultural/multimodal/multisystems approach in working with culturally different families.* Westport, CT: Praeger.

Gopaul-McNicol, S. (1997b). A theoretical framework for training monolingual school psychologists to work with multilingual/multicultural children: An exploration of the major competencies. *Psychology in the Schools, 34*(1), 17–29.

Gopaul-McNicol, S., & Armour Thomas, E. (1997a). A case study on the bio ecological approach to intellectual assessment. *Cultural Diversity and Mental Health, 3*(2), 40–47.

Gopaul-McNicol, S., & Armour-Thomas, E. (1997b). The role of a bio-ecological assessment system in writing a culturally sensitive report: The importance of assessing other intelligences. *Journal of Social Distress and the Homeless, 6*(2), 127–139.

Gopaul-McNicol, S., Black, K., & Clark-Castro, S. (1997). Introduction: Intelligence testing with minority children. *Cultural Diversity and Mental Health, 3*(2), 1–4.

Gopaul-McNicol, S., Thomas, I., & Irish, G. (1991). *A handbook for immigrants: Some basic educational and social issues in the United States of America.* New York: Caribbean Research Center.

Grantham, R. (1996). *Final report of the cultural competence work group.* New York State Office of Mental Health Strategic Plan.

Grier, W., & Cobbs, P. (1968). *Black rage*. New York: Basic Books.

Griffith, E. E. H., & Baker, F. M. (1993). Psychiatric care of African Americans. In A. C. Gaw (Ed.), *Culture, ethnicity and mental illness* (pp. 147–173). Washington, DC: American Psychiatric Press.

Gushue, G., & Sciarra, D. (1995). Culture and families: A multidimensional approach. In J. Ponterotto, J. Casas, L. Suzuki, & C. Alexander (Eds.), *Handbook of multicultural counseling*. Thousand Oaks, CA: Sage.

Halsell Miranda, A. (1993). Consultation with culturally diverse families. *Journal of Educational and Psychological Consultation, 4*(1), 89–93.

Hartman, A. (1978). Diagrammatic assessment of family relationships. *Social Casework, 59,* 465–476.

Hartman, A., & Laird, J. (1983). *Family-centered social work practice*. New York: Free Press.

Helms, J. E. (1985). Cultural identity in the treatment process. In P. Pedersen (Ed.), *Handbook of cross-cultural counseling and therapy*. Westport, CT: Greenwood Press.

Helms, J. E. (1992). Why is there no study of cultural equivalence in standardized cognitive ability testing? *American Psychologist, 47*(9), 1083–1101.

High Achieving Asian Americans are fastest growing minority. (1985, October). *Population Today*, pp. 2, 8.

Hilliard, A. G. (1979). Standardization and cultural bias as impediments to the scientific study and validation of "intelligence." *Journal of Research and Development in Education, 12*(2), 47–58.

Hills, H. I., & Strozier, A. L. (1992). Multicultural training in APA-approved counseling psychology programs: A survey. *Professional Psychology: Research and Practice, 23*(1), 43–51.

Ho, M. K. (1990). *Intermarried couples in therapy*. Springfield, IL: Thomas.

Holman, A. (1983). *Family assessment: Tools for understanding and intervention*. Beverly Hills, CA: Sage.

Homel, P., Palif, M., & Aaronson, D. (Eds.). (1987). *Childhood bilingualism: Aspects of linguistic, cognitive and social development*. Hillsdale, NJ: Erlbaum.

Horn, J. L. (1991). Measurement of intellectual capabilities: A review of theory. In K. S. McGrew, J. W. Werder, & R. W. Woodcock (Eds.), *WJ-R technical manual*. Chicago: Riverside.

Isajiw, W. W. (1990). Ethnic identity retention. In R. Breton, W. W. Isajiw, W. E. Kalbach, & J. G. Reitz (Eds.), *Ethnic identity and equality* (pp. 34–91). Toronto: University of Toronto Press.

Jacobson, E. (1938). *Progressive relaxation*. Chicago: University of Chicago Press.

Jaeger, M. E., & Rosnow, R. L. (1988). Contextualism and its implications for inquiry. *British Journal of Psychology, 79,* 63–75.

Jensen, A. R. (1979). Outmoded theory or unconquered frontier? *Creative Science and Technology, 2,* 16–29.

Johnson, S. D. (1982). *The Minnesota multiethnic counselor education curriculum: The design and evaluation of an intervention for cross-cultural counselor education.* Unpublished doctoral dissertation, University of Minnesota, Minneapolis.

Johnson, S. D. (1987). Knowing that versus knowing how: Towards achieving expertise through multicultural training for counsel. *Counseling Psychologist, 15,* 320–331.

Johnson, S. D. (1990). Towards clarifying culture, race and ethnicity in the context of multicultural counseling. *Journal of Multicultural Counseling and Development, 18,* 4.

Kashani, J. H., Beck, N. C., Heoper, E. W., Fallhi, C., Corcoran, C. M., McAllister, J. A., Rosenberg, T. K., & Reid, J. C. (1987). Psychiatric disorders in a community sample of adolescents. *American Journal of Psychiatry, 144,* 584–589.

Kim, S. C. (1985). Family therapy for Asian Americans: A strategic-structural framework. *Psychotherapy, 22,* 342–348.

Kiselica, M. S. (1991, September/October). Reflections on a multicultural internship experience. *Journal of Counseling and Development, 70,* 126–130.

Korman, M. (1974). National conference on levels and patterns of professional training in psychology: Major themes. *American Psychologist, 29,* 301–313.

Korman, M. (Ed.). (1976). *Levels and patterns of professional training.* Washington, DC: American Psychological Association.

Kouri, K. M., & Lasswell, M. (1993). Black-white marriages: Social change and intergenerational mobility. *Marriage and Family Review, 19,* 241–255.

Landgarten, H. B. (1993). *Magazine photo collage: A multicultural assessment and treatment technique.* New York: Bruner/Mazel.

Lave, J. (1977). Tailor-made experiments and evaluating the intellectual consequences of apprenticeship training. *The Quarterly Newsletter of the Institute for Comparative Human Development, 1,* 1–3.

Lazarus, A. A. (1976). *Multimodal behavior therapy.* New York: Springer.

Lefley, H. P. (1979). Prevalence of potential falling-out cases among Black, Latin and non-white populations of the city of Miami. *Social Science and Medicine, 13B,* 113–128.

Lefley, H. P. (1986). Evaluating the effects of cross-cultural training: Some research results. In H. P. Lefley & P. B. Pedersen (Eds.), *Cross-cultural training for mental health professionals* (pp. 265–307). Springfield, IL: Thomas.

Leininger, M. (1973). Witchcraft practices and psychocultural therapy with urban and United States families. *Human Organizations, 32*(1), 73–83.

Leong, F., & Wagner, N. (1994). Cross-cultural counseling supervision: What do we know? What do we need to know? *Counselor Education and Supervision, 34*(2), 117–131.

Lewis, S. (1994). Cognitive behavioral approaches. In L. Comas-Diaz & B. Greene (Eds.), *Women of color: Integrating ethnic and gender identities in psychotherapy* (pp. 223–238). New York: Guilford Press.

Lidz, C. S. (1991). *Practitioner's guide to dynamic assessment.* New York: Guilford Press.

Marsella, A. J., Kinzie, D., & Gordon, P. (1973). Ethnic variation in the expression of depression. *Journal of Cross-Cultural Psychology, 4,* 435–458.

McGoldrick, M., & Garcia-Preto, N. (1984). Ethnic intermarriage: Implications for therapy. *Family Process, 23,* 347–364.

McGoldrick, M., Pearce, J. K., & Giordano, J. (1982). *Ethnicity and family therapy.* New York: Guilford Press.

McGrew, K. S. (1995). Analysis of the major intelligence batteries according to a proposed comprehensive Gf-Gc framework of human cognitive and knowledge abilities. In D. P. Flanagan, J. L. Genshaft, & P. L. Harrison (Eds.), *Beyond traditional intellectual assessment: Contemporary and emerging theories, tests and issues.* Manuscript submitted for publication.

McNeill, B., Hom, K., & Perez, J. (1995). The training and supervisory needs of racial and ethnic minority students. *Journal of Multicultural Counseling and Development, 23*(4), 246–258.

McNicol, M. (1991). *Helping children adjust to a new culture: A child's perspective.* New York: Multicultural Educational and Psychological Services.

McRae, M. B., & Johnson, S. (1991, September/October). Toward training for competence in multicultural counselor education. *Journal of Counseling and Development, 70,* 131–135.

McRoy, R. G., Freeman, E. G.,Logan, S. L., & Blackmon, B. (1986). Cross-cultural field supervision: Implications for social work education. *Journal of Social Work Education, 22,* 50–56.

Medway, F. (1995). Best practices in assisting families who move and relocate. In A. Thomas & J. Grimes (Eds.), *Best practices in school psychology* (Vol. 3, pp. 977–985). Washington, DC: National Association of School Psychologists.

Meinchenbaum, D. H. (1977). *Cognitive-behavior modification.* New York: Plenum Press.

Mercer, J. R. (1979). In defense of racially and culturally non-discriminatory assessment. *School Psychology Digest, 8*(1), 89–115.

Midgette, T. E., & Meggert, S. S. (1991). Multicultural counseling instruction: A challenge for faculties in the 21st century. *Journal of Counseling and Development, 70,* 136–141.

Minuchin, S. (1974). *Families and family therapy.* Cambridge, MA: Harvard University Press.

Minuchin, S., Montalvo, B., Guerney, B. G., Jr., Rosman, B. L., & Schumer, F. (1967). *Families of the slums.* New York: Basic Books.

Mio, J. S. (1989). Experiential involvement as an adjunct to teaching cultural sensitivity. *Journal of Multicultural Counseling and Development, 17,* 38–46.

Mollica, R. F., Wyshak, G., & Lowelle, J. (1987). The psychosocial impact of war trauma and torture on Southeast Asian refugees. *American Journal of Psychiatry, 144*(12), 1567–1572.

Mosley-Howard, S. (1995). Best practices in considering the of role culture. In A. Thomas & J. Grimes (Eds.), *Best practices in school psychology*

(Vol. 3, pp. 337–345). Washington, DC: National Association of School Psychologists.

Mowder, B. (1980). A strategy for the assessment of bilingual handicapped children. *Psychology in the Schools, 17*(1), 7–11.

Murphy, L. L., Conoley, J. C., & Impara, J. C. (Eds.). (1994). *Tests in Print IV.* Lincoln: University of Nebraska Press.

Murtaugh, M. (1985, Fall). The practice of arithmetic by American grocery shoppers. *Anthropology and Education Quarterly.*

Myers, L. J. (1991). Expanding the psychology of knowledge optimally: The importance of worldview revisited. In R. L. Jones (Ed.), *Black psychology* (3rd ed., pp. 15–28). Berkeley, CA: Cobb & Henry.

Noble, C. E. (1969). Race, reality and experimental psychology. *Perspectives in Biology and Medicine, 13,* 10–30.

Oakland, T. (1977). *Psychological and educational assessment of minority children.* New York: Brunner/Mazel.

Oakland, T., & Phillips, B. N. (1973). *Assessing minority group children.* New York: Behavioral.

Ortiz, A., & Yates, J. R. (1983). Linguistically and culturally diverse handicapped students: Implications for manpower planning. *Journal of the National Association of Bilingual Education, 7*(3), 41–53.

Palmer, D., Hughes, J., & Juarez, L. (1991). School psychology training and the education of at-risk youth: The Texas A & M University program emphasis on handicapped Hispanic children and youth. *School Psychology Review, 21*(4), 603–616.

Paniagua, F. A. (1994). *Assessing and treating culturally diverse clients: A practical guide.* Thousand Oaks, CA: Sage.

Parker, W. M., Valley, M. M., & Geary, C. A. (1986). Acquiring cultural knowledge for counselors in training: A multifaceted approach. *Counselor Education and Supervision, 26,* 61–71.

Payne, M. (1989). Use and abuse of corporal punishment: A Caribbean view. *Child Abuse and Neglect, 13,* 389–401.

Pedersen, P. B. (1973, September). *A cross-cultural coalition training model for educating mental health professionals to function in a multicultural population.* Paper presented at the ninth International Congress of Ethnological and Anthropological Science, Chicago.

Pedersen, P. (1985). *Handbook of cross-cultural counseling and therapy.* Westport, CT: Greenwood Press.

Pedersen, P. (1995). Culture-centered ethical guidelines for counselors. In J. G. Ponterotto, J. M. Casas, L. A. Suzuki, & C. M. Alexander (Eds.), *Handbook of multicultural counseling* (pp. 34–49). Thousand Oaks, CA: Sage.

Philippe, J., & Romain, J. B. (1979). Indisposition in Haiti. *Social Science and Medicine, 13B,* 129–133.

Pinderhughes, E. (1989). *Understanding race, ethnicity and power: The key to efficacy in clinical practice.* New York: Free Press.

Ponterotto, J. G., & Casas, J. M. (1987, April). In search of multicultural competencies within counselor education. *Journal of Counseling and Development, 64*, 430–434.

Ponterotto, J. G., & Casas, J. M. (1991). *Handbook of racial/ethnic minority counseling research*. Springfield, IL: Thomas.

Ponterotto, J. M., Casas, J. M., Suzuki, L. A., & Alexander, C. M. (Eds.). (1995). *Handbook of multicultural counseling*. Thousand Oaks, CA: Sage.

Ponterotto, J. M., Rieger, B., Barrett, A., & Sparks, R. (1994). Assessing multicultural counseling competence: A review of the instrumentation. *Journal of Counseling and Development, 72*, 316–322.

Porterfield, E. (1973, January). Mixed marriage. *Psychology Today*, 71–78.

Porterfield, E. (1982). Black American intermarriage in the United States. *Marriage and Family Review, 5*(1), 17–34.

Ramirez, M., III. (1991). *Psychotherapy and counseling with minorities: A cognitive approach to individual and cultural differences*. New York: Pergamon Press.

Ray, S. (1976). *I deserve love: How affirmations can guide you to personal fulfillment*. Millbrae, CA: Les Femmes.

Ray, S. (1980). *Loving relationships*. Berkeley, CA: Celstial Arts.

Reid, J. (1986, February). Immigration and the future of U.S. Black population. *Population Today, 14*, 6–8.

Remington, G., & DaCosta, G. (1989). Ethnocultural factors in resident supervision: Black supervisor and White supervisees. *American Journal of Psychotherapy, 43*(3), 398–404.

Reynolds, A. (1995). Challenges and strategies for teaching multicultural counseling courses. In J. Ponterotto, J. M. Casas, L. A. Suzuki, & C. M. Alexander (Eds.), *Handbook of multicultural counseling* (pp. 312–330). Thousand Oaks, CA: Sage.

Ridley, C. R. (1985). Imperatives for ethnic and cultural relevance in psychology training programs. *Professional Psychology: Research and Practice, 16*(5), 611–622.

Ridley, C. R. (1995). *Overcoming unintentional racisim in counseling and therapy*. Thousand Oaks, CA: Sage.

Rimer, S. (1991, September 16). Between two worlds: Dominicans in New York. *New York Times*, p. B6-L.

Rodriguez-Fernandez, C. M. (1981). *Testing and the Puerto Rican child: A practical guidebook for psychologists and teachers*. Unpublished doctoral dissertation, University of Massachusetts.

Rogers, M., Close Conoley, J., Ponterotto, J., & Wiese, M. J. (1992). Multicultural training in school psychology: A national survey. *School Psychology Review, 21*(4), 603–616.

Rogoff, B. (1978). Spot observations: An introduction and examination. *Quarterly Newsletter of the Institute for Comparative Human Development, 2*, 21–26.

Rogoff, B., & Chavajay, P. (1995). What's become of research on the cultural basis of intellectual development? *American Psychologist, 50*(10), 859–877.

Ronstrom, A. (1989). Children in Central America: Victims of war. *Child Welfare League of America, 58*(2), 145–153.

Rosenblatt, P., Karis, T., & Powell, R. (1995). *Multiracial couples: Black and white voices.* Thousand Oaks, CA: Sage.

Ruble, A. J., O'Nell, C. W., & Collado-Ardon, R. (1984). *Susto: A folk illness.* Berkeley: University of California Press.

Sabnani, H. B., Ponterotto, J. G., & Borodovsky, L. G. (1991). White racial identity development and cross-cultural counselor training: A stage model. *The Counseling Psychologist, 19*(1), 76–102.

Saeki, C., & Borow, H. (1987). Counseling and psychotherapy: East and West. In P. Pedersen (Ed.), *Handbook of cross-cultural counseling and therapy* (pp. 223–229). New York: Praeger.

Samuda, R. (1975). From ethnocentrism to a multicultural perspective in educational testing. *Journal of Afro-American Issues, 3*(1), 4–17.

Samuda, R. (1976). Problems and issues in assessment of minority group children. In R. L. Jones (Ed.), *Mainstreaming and the minority child* (pp. 65–76). Reston, VA: Council for Exceptional Children.

Shon, S. P., & Ja, D. Y. (1982). Asian families. In M. McGoldrick, J. K. Pearce, & J. Giordano (Eds.), *Ethnicity and family therapy* (pp. 123–133). New York: Guilford Press.

Simons, R. C., & Hughes, C. C. (1993). Culture-bound syndromes. In A. C. Gaw (Ed.), *Culture, ethnicity, and mental illness*(pp. 75–93). Washington, DC: American Psychiatric Press.

Skinner, B. F. (1974). *About behaviorism.* New York: Knopf.

Sloan, T. S. (1990). Psychology for the third world. *Journal of Social Issues, 46*(3), 1–20.

Sodowsky, G. R., Kwan, K. K., & Pannu, R. (1995). Ethnic identity of Asians in the United States. In J. G. Ponterotto, J. M. Casas, L. A. Suzuki, & C. M. Alexander (Eds.), *Handbook of multicultural counseling* (pp. 123–154). Thousand Oaks, CA: Sage.

Sternberg, R. J. (1984, January). What should intelligence tests test? Implications of a triarchic theory of intelligence for intelligence testing. *Educational Researcher,* 5–15.

Sternberg, R. J. (1986). *Intelligences applied.* New York: Harcourt Brace Jovanovich.

Sternberg, R. J., Wagner, R. K., & Okagaki, L. (1993). Practical intelligence: The nature and role of tacit knowledge in work and at school. In H. Reese & J. Puckett (Eds.), *Advances in lifespan development* (pp. 205–227). Hillsdale, NJ: Erlbaum.

Sue, D. (1981). *Counseling the culturally different: Theory and practice.* New York: Wiley.

Sue, D., Arredondo, P., & McDavis, R. (1992). Multicultural counseling competencies and standards: A call to the profession. *Journal of Multicultural Counseling and Development, 20,* 64–88.

Sue, D. W., & Sue, D. (1990). *Counseling the culturally different: Theory and practice* (2nd ed.). New York: Wiley.

Sue, S., & Zane, N. (1987, January). The role of culture and cultural techniques in psychotherapy. *American Psychologist, 42,* 37–45.

Super, C. M. (1980). Cognitive development: Looking across at growing up. In C. Super & M. Harkness (Eds.), *New Directions for Child Development: Anthropological Perspectives on Child Development, 8,* 59–69.

Suzuki, L. A., & Kugler, J. F. (1995). Intelligence and personality assessment. In J. G. Ponterotto, J. M. Casas, L. A. Suzuki, & C. M. Alexander (Eds.), *Handbook of multicultural counseling* (pp. 493–515). Thousand Oaks, CA: Sage.

Suzuki, L. A., Meller, P. J., & Ponterotto, J. G. (Eds.). (1996). *Handbook of multicultural assessment.* San Francisco: Jossey-Bass.

Tapp, J. L., Kelman, H., Triandis, H., Wrightsman, L., & Coelho, G. (1974). Advisory principles for ethical considerations in the conduct of cross-cultural research: Fall 1973 revision. *International Journal of Psychology, 9,* 231–349.

Thomas, T. (1991, August). *Post traumatic stress disorder in children.* Paper presented at the annual meeting of the American Psychological Association, Boston.

Thomas, T., & Gopaul-McNicol, S. (1991). *An immigrant handbook on special education in the United States of America.* New York: Multicultural Educational and Psychological Services.

Thrasher, S., & Anderson, G. (1988, March). The West Indian family: Treatment challenges. *Social Casework. Journal of Contemporary Social Work,* 171–176.

Thurstone, L. L. (1924). *The nature of intelligence.* New York: Harcourt Brace.

Triandis, H. (1987). Some major dimensions of cultural variation in client populations. In P. Pedersen (Ed.), *Handbook of cross-cultural counseling and therapy* (pp. 21–28). New York: Praeger.

Tseng, W., Xu, D., Ebata, K., Hsu, J., & Cul, Y. (1986). Diagnostic pattern for neuroses among China, Japan and America. *American Journal of Psychiatry, 143,* 1010–1014.

Tucker, J. A. (1980). *Nineteen steps for assuring non-biased placement of students in special education.* Reston, VA: ERIC Clearinghouse on Handicapped and Gifted Children.

Turner, P. A. (1994). *Ceramic uncles and celluloid mammies: Black images and their influence in culture.* New York: Bantam/Doubleday.

U.S. Department of Commerce News. (1989, October 12). *Hispanic Population surpasses 20 million mark; grows by 39 percent, census bureau reports.* Census Bureau Press Release. (CB 89-58).

Vygotsky, L. S. (1978). *Mind in society: The development of higher psychological processes.* Cambridge, MA: Harvard University Press.

Wechsler, D. (1958). *The measurement and appraisal of adult intelligence* (4th ed.). Baltimore: Williams & Wilkins.

Westermeyer, J. J. (1993). Cross-cultural psychiatric assessment. In A. C. Gaw (Ed.), *Culture, ethnicity, and mental illness* (pp. 125–144). Washington, DC: American Psychiatric Press.

Wittkower, E. D. (1964). Spirit possession in Haitain voodoo ceremonies. *Acta Psychother, 12*, 72–80.

Wolpe, J. (1969). *The practice of behavior therapy.* Oxford, England: Pergamon Press.

Woodcock, R. E. (1990). Theoretical foundations of the WJ-R measures of cognitive ability. *Journal of Psychoeducational Assessment, 8*, 231–258.

Wrenn, C. G. (1985). Afterward: The culturally encapsulated counselor revisited. In P. Pedersen (Ed.), *Handbook of cross-cultural counseling and therapy* (pp. 323–329). Westport, CT: Greenwood Press.

Wright, E. (Ed.). (1992). *Feminism and psychoanalysis.* Oxford, England: Blackwell.

Index